Books by Lazaris

IN ENGLISH

Lazaris Blank Journals
The Sacred Journey: You and Your Higher Self
The Sirius Connection
Working with Your Shadow: An Imperative on the Spiritual Path

IN JAPANESE

The Sacred Journey: You and Your Higher Self

IN GERMAN

The Sacred Journey: You and Your Higher Self

IN SPANISH

Lazaris Interviews: Book I
Lazaris Interviews: Book II
The Sacred Journey: You and Your Higher Self

LAZARIS

The Sirius Connection

NPN Publishing, Inc.
P. O. Box 3285, Palm Beach, FL 33480

LAZARIS

The Sirius Connection

Cover art, *"Gateway to Sirius,"* © 1994 by Gilbert Williams.
A full-color poster is available from Concept: Synergy, 1-800/678-2356.

© 1996 NPN Publishing, Inc.
P. O. Box 3285, Palm Beach, FL 33480
1-800/678-2356

1st Printing 1996

Photographs by Michaell North

ISBN 1-55638-301-0

Dedication

This book is dedicated to Peny,
the one we came to touch,
the one who truly touches us.
We love you.

— Lazaris

THE LAZARIS MAILING LIST

To be placed on Lazaris' mailing list, please call or write Concept: Synergy, 1-800/678-2356 (561/642-2399 from overseas), P. O. Box 3285, Palm Beach, FL 33480.

LAZARIS ...

For as long as there is Light ...

"We are here to remind you that pain and fear are not the only methods of growth, that you can more elegantly grow through joy and love ... that you do create your own reality ... that there is a God/Goddess/All That Is who loves you, who knows your name ... and that you love — you love 'good enough.'

"For as long as there is Light ... and the Light is forever ... we shall love you."

— Lazaris

Since 1974 Lazaris has channeled through Jach Pursel, his only channel, offering his friendship and love and generating a remarkable body of tools, techniques, processes, and pathways for our Spiritual Journey Home to God/Goddess/All That Is.

He has touched thousands in his extraordinary workshops, and tens of thousands more with the books, video tapes, and audio tapes that many have said are the finest tools of metaphysics and spirituality available.

We invite you to explore the Love, the Light, the Joy, and the Wonder which is the Spark of Love known as Lazaris.

A Note about Lazaris' Use of Language

Throughout this book Lazaris refers to himself as "we." Ever since he began communicating with us in 1974, he has done that. Lazaris says that each of us has many selves, but that right now we are experiencing them one at a time, and thus we refer to ourselves as "I." Lazaris has many selves as well — many selves in many dimensions — but experiences them all simultaneously and therefore refers to himself as "we." It is not the use of the "parental we" or the "editorial we," but rather a reflection of Lazaris' experience of his own reality.

Also, often you will find that Lazaris will use a plural pronoun or modifier in a place you might expect to find a singular one. This is done to avoid using the generic masculine pronouns which tend to make women feel as if they are not included in what is being said. To make certain they do know they are included, Lazaris often uses plural pronouns which, though against the rules, are better aligned with what is true.

Finally, much of the material in this book is taken from several seminars — a weekend and several one-day workshops. In preparing the material for publication, we have retained in the written form indications of audience response which do much to pass along the resonance of safety, warmth, humor, and love which Lazaris created in talking about this topic.

Contents

The Sirius Connection

Resources

The following Lazaris tapes are helpful in working with some of the issues in this chapter or offer further exploration of related areas:

> *Creating a Brilliant Future*
> *Secrets To Changing Anything in Your Life — Instantly*
> *The Future: How To Create It*

1

The Great Work Calls You

The Great Work calls you to be committed enough to stand up, to take a stand upon your beliefs and upon your truths. And from that lofty and sometimes precarious pinnacle, it calls you to stretch and to reach for even higher truths and more freeing beliefs.

Let us show you a world you've not yet seen — a world more real that will amaze and thrill you. Come, let us hold your hand and steady your stance upon your pinnacle as you reach for even more — as you allow The Dream to triumph. Let the Great Work unfold.

— Lazaris

There is a wondrous and mysterious love that is beyond all words, all language, and all sound. Yet in the silence, it can be heard in every heart and can fill every mind. Love yourself enough to listen.

— Lazaris

Whether your metaphysical-spiritual journey is a few months old or many years old, with increasing eagerness and increasing enthusiasm, each of you has sought that elusive essence called power and strength. Each of you has sought that mysterious essence called talent. And whether your growth is a few months or many years, you have learned the words. More, you have learned a magic that can transmute, that can transform those very words into action.

And you know that you are powerful. You know that you are strong. Even as you are reluctant to admit it, even as you are reticent to use it, you know that you have power.

More than words, you have the ability — you have the magic — to turn thoughts and feelings into creations and manifestations and to turn words into actions.

You know that you have talent. You do not always know how to use that power, that strength, that talent — you do not always know what they are going to produce. But you know — somewhere deep inside you, you know — of your strength, power, and talent. Yes, you do.

And as that knowing becomes increasingly conscious, you also come to know that having power, strength, and talent is not enough. Even using power, strength, and talent is not enough. It isn't enough.

The Great Work — what we have come to call The Great Work — is the work of becoming more and more conscious. It is the work of using your power, your strength, and your talent to make a better way for yourself, to center yourself. But it's more than that. It is using that very power, strength, talent — however eloquently or haltingly defined, however strong or weak you think or know it is — to make a better reality not only for yourself but also for those you love, for those you care about, and for your world.

The Great Work is the work of taking that which you have to create a future, but not just any future: It is taking what you have to create a positive future of dreams.

So many are eager to tell you there is no future. Some among them are so enthusiastic about convincing themselves (and hopefully you) that there is no future at all. They are convinced that what is to come is only doom and gloom. Often this is because they — the "Doomers and Gloomers" — cannot think of a solution; they cannot find the answers. The narrowness of their logic and reasoning concludes that if they cannot find a solution or if they do not know the answer, there is no solution, and there is no answer. The only solution or answer is destruction. They reason that the only solution is to wipe the slate of reality clean and to start over.

The Great Work is to swim in a different way, to create a different future, to create a positive future of dreams — — in spite of all that, despite the direction of the flow.

But the Great Work is more than that. The Great Work involves activity and utilizing your power with its force, in conjunction and combination with your strengths and your talents, to create a field of force — a force field — out of which to give birth to what we have called the Virgin Future. We say it again: The Great Work is the work that accesses a unique force field to participate in the midwifery of birthing a future "untouched by human hands" — a Virgin Future. It is using that power and force, using that strength, using that talent to create a force field — a field of force, if you will — that can also give birth to what we call a Virgin Future.

Forever there have been a myriad of futures available, from the worst to the very best. There has been a vast array, a spray of futures, from which you could choose. And as you would become more and more conscious, you would choose.

But just over a decade ago, among that array, among that spray of possible futures, there was a new seed, a tiny speck, that showed up that was not there before. A tiny seed of a future, that had not been conceived before, suddenly showed up. A future that previously could not be conceived — it was, before that time, impossible — suddenly became a part of the array.

This potential Virgin Future could not have been seen by the pundits, the seers, and the prophets of the past no matter how clear their vision was. It could not be seen because this particular seed did not exist until the early 1980s.

The Great Work is the work of conceiving and perceiving. It is the work of understanding and of gathering

We say it again: The Great Work is the work that accesses a unique force field to participate in the midwifery of birthing a future "untouched by human hands" — a Virgin Future.

and giving meaning. This new seed is still in the process of being conceived and of being perceived. So much has not even begun of the understanding and of the gathering and giving of meaning.

The Great Work is conceiving this Virgin Future, and then it is to carry this future in the womb of Being. The midwifery that assists the birth deals with the perceiving, the understanding, and the meaning. For it is you — Mapmaker, Dreamer, and Dreamweaver — who is to give birth to this Virgin Future. It is a part of your destiny; it is part of why you are here.

The Virgin Future, truly a future of magic and miracles, is more and is different from the positive future of dreams about which we have so often spoken. This never-before-conceived future is one where the problems do not have to be fixed or solved; they have been changed, healed, and resolved. Oh, there is so much more.

But it is not ours to tell you of this Virgin Future and of the New World that it can create. For you are about your Great Work. You are about founding, not finding, a new spirituality. You are about creating that Virgin Future in accordance with your destiny — in accordance with your design and direction.

Know that the seed has been planted and that a Virgin Future with a New World is there amid and among the possibilities. What was not possible, now is. And it is yours to make it so. That is the Great Work that you are about.

It is time to be about your Great Work. As we have said for several years now: Practice is over. You are no longer a practicing metaphysician: You are a living magician. Practice is over.

When you practice your metaphysics and spirituality, when you are content to practice, you live in a world in which you will always respond to external events, learning the lessons in hindsight — a valuable sight, a clear sight, use it! — always learning retrospectively, retroactively. You continue the dance of remembering and forgetting.

Do not be content with practice. When you are, you live in a world of problem-solving with the constant threat that you have finally come upon the problem you cannot solve — you live in a world where problem-solving becomes crisis-resolving, with the continuing threat that you have stumbled into the crisis that cannot be resolved.

When instead of practicing you will live your metaphysics, when you will accept the artistry as well as the skill of being a metaphysician, then you can stop chasing your spirituality and start living it. What has been too elusive can become illuminating, and you can have a solidity of a relationship and a partnership with your Higher Self, with your Soul, with your Spirit, with God, with the Goddess, with All That Is — and with God/Goddess/All That Is.

You stop chasing after such a relationship and partnership. You start living, breathing, embracing, loving it.

With the artistry of being, your world starts responding to you — and you, step by step, stop reacting to the world. When you accept that you are the metaphysician, the spiritual being, you get off the dance floor of remembering and forgetting ... 1-2-3, 1-2-3 dip ... {laughter} ... and remembering becomes a knowing in which your first response is metaphysical, your first response is spiritual. And it becomes the only response because it answers, it responds wholly.

When you accept the artistry, yes, there will still be problems to be solved, there will still be crises to be resolved, but the resolutions will be done with an elegance and an ease. You — with the integrity that holds the space within for every part of self — will become a deeper, richer, riper self. You will become more of yourself and more able to be about the Great Work.

Even though practice is over and we encourage you not to be content with only practice, please also understand: You do not have time to become totally powerful. You do not have to be the best metaphysician-magician. Practically, you do not have time to become totally successful or to become the best magician. ... {laughter} ...

...then you can stop chasing your spirituality and start living it. What has been too elusive can become illuminating...

Maybe it would be nice if you did, but you have neither the time nor the space. You have to go with what you've got. And you have enough. You are enough. You are enough.

You are enough, and you are not alone. You do not have to do it alone. There is help. There is grand help that is so available. You have all the Light and all the Information that you need to move beyond practice, to be the metaphysician-magician, and to be about the Great Work you came to do.

Remember … within the Great Work there is untold energy and undefined force, and that energy with its force can create a unique force field of your power, strength, and talent. You can ignite and forge that energy and that force. It can work for you; it can catapult you forward upon your path and upon your journey.

You see, this is why it does not matter if you do not have all the power you could possibly have. You can go with what you have, even if you are not sure it is enough — even if you are not sure you are enough.

And you are not alone; there is help. The Goddess is returning, though She never left. She is returning and with Her she brings a Light. She brings Her Light.

The Vortex of Sirius opens each year on July 23rd. The Vortex of Sirius opened in a way that it has never opened in over 90,000 years on April 23, 1994. It opened full and wide — a Grand Opening of Sirius. Through the Vortex came a flood of Light and a flood of Information — Her Light and all the information you need to be about the Great Work and all that attends it.

Let us explore your connection to Sirius. Let us explore your Sirius Connection …

Celebrate your Great Work! Open your heart wide and full, filling it with love and celebration. Then your Spirit can rise on the winds of change, billowing with clearer thought, surging with creativity and intuition, swirling with more potent choice.

— Lazaris

Resources

The following Lazaris tapes are helpful in working with some of the issues in this chapter or offer further exploration of related areas:

The Goddess: Beginning To Receive Her
Harmony: The Power Vortex
Balance: Releasing the Full Self

2

Vortex of the Goddess: Birth of a Universe

Miracles are the subtle wisps and whispers that God and Goddess are at play in your reality and within your reality creations and manifestations. Often they seem to come "out of the blue" — often, out of the blue light of Sirius — as magic.

A Miracle Worker and a Mapmaker, you can come to consciously create — to actively make — miracles. When you do, you become a bit more of the god-being that you were always meant to be — that you have always been. And you come a little closer to Home.

— Lazaris

Your universe, as we have suggested many times, as we've suggested already this morning, is but one universe among many. It is relatively a small universe — not to suggest that you should feel badly ... {laughter} ... for despite the consensus reality that bigger is better, despite the male-dominating energy and the comparative energies that say "bigger is better," your universe, though relatively small, is not at all diminished by its size.

Now we know the word universe by its definition means the totality of known or supposed objects and phenomena throughout space. We know that it is thought of as "all" and that therefore there can only be one. Yet, by experience and by fact, yours is but one among many dimensional and non-dimensional universes. Yours is a universe by a truer definition: It is that which is *versus* (turning into) *uni* (one). Universe.

And it is mostly space, as you know. And it is mostly outer space as you call it. Before anything, your universe is space. Space. What about before space?

To understand the Vortex of Sirius and the Sirius Connection, realize that before your universe existed, before it was even conceived, there was nothing. First space had to be created. As with any dimensional creation, first comes space.

We have suggested that the Goddess energy — the original energy that creates itself without space or time — first creates God. No, we do not mean the God of religious text and doctrine Eastern or Western — not that God that so frequently comes to mind when the word is said or thought. We speak of the genuine article, if you will. We speak of the more-real God that to most remains unknown.

The Goddess first creates God. She first gives birth to God, if you will, from her womb. The egg of new form, fertilized by the new spark of Her Light, gives birth to that energy — spaceless energy — that is God.

Why? So that together Goddess and God can continuously create — give birth to — All That Is. Together. Together, we would suggest, because the Goddess has no desire to be the singular authority. She has no desire to have singular supremacy or to be singularly supreme. She has no desire to be absolute. She does want to work together. She always does.

In the context of your language, and thus in the context of your time, the Goddess first created God so that God with Goddess could create All That Is. The Goddess created the spaceless-space, and then She created the manifestation of the formless-form, if you will, of God.

She could have gone on and created all space and all manifestation to fill that space. She could have done that on her own and by Herself. But She did not want to.

Instead, as we say, She wanted to do it together. As She desired (and desires still), God and Goddess together gave birth to All That Is. It happened and is always happening. It always will. Out of this "was, is, and will be" a synergy emerges. The whole is greater than the sum of its parts. God/Goddess/All That Is is that whole.

Feminine energy never wants to be singular or supreme. That's something that masculine energy, in its dominating principle, cannot grok. ... {laughter} ... Whether expressed in the male form or the female form, that dominating masculine energy just cannot ... "What do you mean she doesn't want to be supreme or singular? Of course, she does. Everybody does. That's the way the world works."

Dominating masculine energy just cannot grok ... "Wait a minute ... ." Startled and stunned, such dominating energy cannot grok it. Even so, feminine energy, genuine feminine — the whole of feminine energy — has no desire to do it alone.

The Goddess has no desire to be the singular authority, to be the one and only God, who loves you and who will kill you if you don't believe it ... {laughter} ... who is all-powerful, but cannot seem to reach you if you slip the slightest bit so that you could be totally dominated and controlled by the Devil. ... {laughter} ... The Goddess has no such desire. She wants to work together.

She begins all her creation by creating space. To create your universe, a universe of free will, first she had to create space. And so in the fabric, if you will, in the fabric of nothing, through a tiny opening, She blew a bubble. ... Now we're talking figuratively here, please! ... {laughter} ... We're talking poetically, because there are no words to describe what we're attempting to describe ... {laughter} ...

Out of nothing, She created a bubble through a tiny tear, if you will, through a tiny rip. ... She created space.

Feminine energy never wants to be singular or supreme. That's something that masculine energy, in its dominating principle, cannot grok. ... {laughter} ...

11

She created a vastness that is beyond anything you can imagine or believe, beyond anything that you can conceive. She created a mighty and majestic vastness that seems as if it is everything — as if it is all that is. It seems as if there could be nothing more.

Yet beyond this rip, beyond this tear, and beyond this bubble, there are other rips and tears that likewise seem as if ... She blew many bubbles.

This tear, this rip, through which She created the space that is your universe, is what we call the Vortex of the Goddess — the Vortex of Sirius. It speaks to what we call the Sirius Connection. It is the portal, the doorway, through which all energy flows into your universe. It is first the tear itself; it is then all the mystery and mysticism that connects you to that tear and to the bubble that is nothing within nothing — that is shimmering space.

It is into this still pond that then enter all the seeds of energy, like tiny little ball bearings, like tiny little pebbles, grains of sand, that have been tossed, tossed into this tranquility, into this stillness. All the seeds begin filling the space. These tiny specks of nothing that are raw energy without form begin to fill the space. And they become fertile with possibility and potential. Impregnated, they begin to grow. In this sea of nothing, scattered throughout it, in every part of it, they begin to grow. A universe has begun as one space — one shimmering bubble — and it continues turning and turning in order to turn into one, once again.

This universe is a shimmering bubble of free will floating in a torus of space-time. It is a shimmering sphere that seems to function as a dimensional hologram.

Holographic photography operates on similar principles as traditional photography, yet in more sophisticated ways. Rather than exposing the film to ordinary light, holographic film is exposed to laser light — to a laser light that is both aimed at and reflected onto film. This laser light, a singular beam of intense light, is split in what is called a ... splitter. ... {laughter} ... Part of that light, a piece of that light called a reference beam, strikes the film. It strikes it like a billion ball bearings striking a still pond, creating ripples wherever they hit, ripples that extend and run into and counterbalance each other, creating an interference pattern.

The other part of the beam has been split off and is sent in a different direction, where it hits an object which is the focus of what you want to photograph. It bounces off that object and is reflected back to the film, but from a different angle. This light also hits the film like thousands of tiny — billions of little tiny — ball bearings. Upon this already-disrupted piece of film, the reflected light creates its own rippling energy. To the naked eye holographic film looks like a bunch of ripples — big ripples, little ripples, some more intense, some less intense. It looks like an interference pattern, like a mishmosh, like nothing at all. Chaos.

But when you look at that holographic film from a certain angle and with a certain intensity of light, out of this rippling, out of this interference pattern, emerges a three-dimensional image, a three-dimensional illusion that you can view from all sides. If you try to touch it, you realize it's not solid. It is an illusion — with a certain degree of opacity — but it is an illusion. An illusion.

Now, what you also know is that upon this same film, you can project another beam that is split into another reference and reflection. It will also scatter all over the film — all over this same piece of film. When you hold the film at one angle, you will see the first image. If you shift the film slightly, you will see the second image, and a third and a fourth — as many images as have been captured upon the film.

In fact, your researchers now know that on a single piece of film no more than one inch square that you could put all the information contained in 300,000 - 400,000 pages of a book. All can be fit onto a piece of film the size of a postage stamp. And you can see all the different information there just by adjusting the angle of viewing and the intensity of light.

You also know that each piece of this film contains all the data, all the information — though more vague and less clear — of the entire film. So if you had only a quarter of this piece of film, you could reconstruct the whole of the film and every one of the images upon it.

Now, imagine that our film is not one inch square but a tiny sphere. Imagine that our film is a shimmering bubble.

When those seeds of energy began filling the space — began landing within the bubble that is your universe — they created interference patterns, ripples. None of them were "visible." Some were elliptical; others, symmetrical. They began to "fill the space."

Out of the interference patterns that are everywhere and nowhere at once, standing waves emerge. Resonance emerges. As energy flows through these interference and resonance patterns, it takes formation and, in time, it becomes information: molecular, gaseous, matter. You call them galaxies. One such spiraling formation you call the Milky Way. It is spiraling energies that are traces of the energy that is invisible.

In your latest high-tech spy movies, there are security systems with ultraviolet light and infrared light that cannot be seen. The light is in formation, but it is invisible. However, the shrewd spies have particular spritzers, and they can … (spritzing sound) … In the dust are the tracings — the tracks of light. They still cannot see the ultraviolet or infrared light, but they can see the reflection and expression — they can see the traces — of that light. "Aha! There's a beam of light."

Out of the interference patterns that are everywhere and nowhere at once, standing waves emerge. Resonance emerges.

So … the seemingly infinite number of stars and the seemingly endless phenomena and anomalies suddenly show up, reflecting what cannot be seen, the energy patterns, sometimes elliptical, sometimes symmetrical.

You haven't seen all the galaxies yet. You haven't "spritzed" enough of the universe. … {laughter} … You know there is yours. Your Milky Way is sitting very much at the edge of this bubble. And at the very edge of this Milky Way, there's this star that you call the sun. And it has these strange bodies called planets that are elliptically orbiting about it. And some of them have moons. It's called the solar system, and the fourth body, the third planet out, is called Earth.

And if you look from Earth, through your galaxy in a particular direction, there is a particular star that has been given the name Sirius. There. That star, so close, so bright — only eight and a half light years away — is Sirius. It is aligned with the portal. It is that portal, therefore, through which all energy has flowed and is flowing into the whole of your universe.

Even though it appears that energy is exploding outward because it is traveling outward at a phenomenal speed — even though the energy appears to have started in the "center" of the universe and is moving outward (Big Bang) — that is not really how it works. Energy is being "drawn" from somewhere outside itself. It appears that energy is moving from the inside to the outside, but more truthfully, it is being attracted. Drawn, not driven; compelled, not propelled. Though appearing as an explosion, it must also be understood as an implosion. Energy, and thus your universe, is being pulled by the Attractor, the Grand Attractor, the Ultimate Attractor, by the Goddess.

It is through this portal that is called Sirius — it is through this gateway represented by the brilliant blue-white star Sirius — that all the energy enters your universe. It is through this doorway that the Grand and Ultimate Attractor enters. It is through this portal and gateway that the Goddess enters your universe. It is Her vortex: The Vortex of Sirius.

No, it's not a physical gateway. If you flew out there, you would not see an opening that you could kind of "look through" ... {laughter} ... but it's there. Etherically, it's there. Beyond the dimensions of length, width, and breadth (one, two, and three) and beyond the dimension of space-time (four) into that fifth dimension and beyond there is a portal through which all energy has come into your universe.

You see, and as we talk of a holographic piece of film that is flat — two-dimensional — your scientists are exploring and learning to project holography onto spherical film — onto bubbles. The analogy works to describe what your universe is: It is a spherical holographic illusion. It is a holographic image expressed as interference patterns which, when looked at from a certain view, from a certain angle, and with a particular intensity of light, appears as a dimensional reality.

Into this holography, through the Vortex of Sirius, comes energy — the energy that is Goddess and that is God/Goddess/All That Is. Through the Vortex of Sirius comes the energy that is your very Soul and Spirit. Also there comes the energy of your Higher Self and of your Real Self, Truer Self — Transcendent Self.

Self creates a holographic brain to project a holographic body which references and reflects itself. Through the holograms of brain and body, Self creates a spherical hologram that you call physical reality. It is a bubble, a shimmering bubble. As with your universe, so your personal universe is as a bubble.

And this bubble isn't that big, either. This bubble is just a quarter inch or less beyond your fingertips. ... {laughter} ... It moves faster than you. You can never touch it; no matter how adept and stealthy you are, you will never touch it.

"I'm going to move that way." ... {laughter} .. It knows. ...{laughter} ... However fast you run, however high you jump, it's always just beyond your fingertips. And upon this bubble you project your reality and the reality of your world.

Another analogy: You now have certain theaters that have huge curved screens. You sit in what appears to be the middle and the screen wraps above, below, left, and right. The lights dim and the projector rolls ... "Wow!" It looks as if you are right in the middle of everything. Now in such theaters they show things like roller coaster rides as you sit there. And it seems so real. It seems so much more real when the screen is curved above, below, to the left and to the right. You look this way, you look that way. It is all around you. It seems so very real.

If you look behind you ... you see ... well, they haven't figured that one out yet. ... {laughter} ...

The energy of your holographic universe flows through the Vortex of Sirius. At a certain point in your growth, when you are done — when you are complete with the physical plane and with the astral, causal and mental planes as well — you, as energy, will exit this universe through that very Vortex of the Goddess. Exit ... into oblivion? ... into nothing? No, into a majestic and mighty vastness that is even more.

This Vortex was closed down over 90,000 years ago. Let us be clear: It was not shut off, only closed down. If it had been shut off, your universe and every energy within it would have ceased and either evaporated or withered. It would be no more. The Vortex was not shut off, but it was closed down. A trickle of its energy flowing, the Vortex of Sirius opens cyclically to flow more fully, more richly and powerfully.

This star system, which is represented by a star called Sirius — the brightest star in your heavens — was known by the ancients and is known in the "primitive" societies of your modern world. The Dogon tribe in northern Africa (as well as many other tribes in Africa) and aboriginal tribes in Australia, South America, and Asia also have knowledge of this star — this singular star, so it appears, that is brighter and seems to twinkle more than other stars.

The ancients knew that around this brilliant star that is Sirius is a dwarf star, a "shadow star," a black star that is much smaller, and more intense, and orbits in an elliptic every 50+ years, causing Sirius to wobble, and appear, therefore, to sparkle more brightly than any other star. All stars sparkle, but none as this one.

And those ancient tribes not only knew it was there, but knew of its 50+ year cycle, and that that cycle was elliptical, not circular. And they have in their ancient records drawings of the movement of Sirius and of the dwarf star Sirius B, laid from a three-dimensional reality into a two-dimensional representation.

They knew that Sirius was the source of all life, of all energy, long before the scientists who replaced the mystics ever speculated anything about it, long before any equip-

Before the ancients of your world who are often dismissed with that singular word "primitive," there was Lemuria, the Land That Imagination Forgot.

ment existed that could measure it, long before your modern world could know.

Before the ancients of your world who are often dismissed with that singular word "primitive," there was Lemuria, the Land That Imagination Forgot. So often we have spoken of Lemuria and the Lemurians that so many of you once were. It was a land located in what you now call the Pacific Ocean. It vanished. When its work was done, it left, not because it was conquered, not because it was destroyed — which in the consensus seems the only way anything could come to an end — but because it was. Lemuria and the Lemurians left by choice. They slipped into the mist from whence they came. By choice.

While Lemurians were present in your world, the Lemurian year revolved around Sirius. The first day of the Lemurian year began on what you now call July 23rd with the Rise of Sirius. That is the day when Sirius rises on your horizon just before the Sun. This brilliant light is immediately swamped, swallowed up by the fires of the Sun, yet an opening has begun. The Rise of Sirius begins a 55-day cycle — July 23 to September 15 — when the Vortex is opened and more fully and widely than at other times. The universe is renewed. It is a time of beginning more profound than spring.

Lemurians geared their entire mysticism, their entire year, their entire cycling of growth to that star, its rise, and the days of its beginning and opening.

Understand: Even though it was closed down over 90,000 years ago and only opens cyclically each year, Sirius is available every day of each year. She did not forsake you; She did not forget you. However, during the Sirius Days — from its rise on July 23 until September 15 — the energy of Sirius is more available and more potent.

Atlantis, likewise, is lost of myth, certainly so. Located in the Atlantic, but lost in myth, many argue: Did it really exist? It will never be proved, but nonetheless it was certainly there, and it, too, aligned itself to Sirius.

The ancients in the Land of Sumer, who created an amazingly advanced civilization, recount the mysteries of

Sirius in their tales. Their civilization is often overlooked or even dismissed by academicians in favor of Egyptian Civilization. Most cannot understand the Land of Sumer, between the Tigris and Euphrates Rivers, or the texts and knowledge of the Sumerians. Even so, in the Land of Sumer, Sirius was the core, the base, of those texts and that knowledge.

And in Egypt, yes, so much revolved around Sirius as Her gateway and as the center of all that is sacred. The pyramids — not really tombs as so many academicians still contend — were temples and monuments of the celestial bodies. They were temples to the Goddess and to Sirius, Her gateway and portal — the gateway and portal.

The Great Pyramid of Cheops aligned with all directions, aligned to the east, aligned to the rise of Sirius. The chambers that have been found and the ones yet to be discovered and explored are strategically positioned in reference and deference to Sirius and all that the Vortex represents. Whatever else the pyramids may be, they are also monuments to the stars — monuments to Sirius. All the mythologies of Isis, Osiris, and Horus in Egypt — and the mythologies in the more ancient Land of Sumer — are based upon this Sirius Connection.

In your modern world, many of the myths are only held alive in the Old Wives Tales ... and even those are now being lost to the younger generations. But some of you are old enough to remember your mother's or grandmother's warning about the Dog Days of Summer, right? July 23 to September 15, the Dog Days of Summer. For reasons long since forgotten, these were special days of cleansing and purifying; they were special days of readying and preparation for the days of harvest — for the days of bounty — that would follow. The Dog Days of Summer correspond to the mystical cycle of the Dog Star constellation — to the magical Days of Sirius.

During those days, the Vortex of Sirius — the Vortex of the Goddess — opens, and an energy of cleansing, purifying, readying, and preparing flows into your universe and into your world. The Vortex opens more than usual, and a flow that is more than a trickle happens.

It happens every day of the year, absolutely, but in those days it happens more powerfully and more profoundly. This cycle of the Rise of Sirius and of the Sirius Days has been happening for tens of thousands of years.

And now, everything is different. ...

Allow yourself the Ultimate Adventure: Rediscover how completely loved you are by God/Goddess/All That Is and how deep is your own capacity to love. ... Let the Journey begin. ... Let it be.

— Lazaris

Resources

The following Lazaris tapes are helpful in working with some of the issues in this chapter or offer further exploration of related areas:

Underlying Truths Assuring Elegance and Ease in 1995
Underlying Truths: Magical Formulas To Master 1996
Chakra Link: You and Your Higher Self
Renewing Chakras
The Magic of Receiving: A New Dimension of Success

3

April 23, 1994:
Opening of the Vortex

Though She never really left, She is returning. The Goddess is returning. She brings a Light — a Divine Light — that is beyond any words, beyond any sound. Yet it can be heard and felt in every heart. She is returning, and She brings a Light. ...

— Lazaris

Let yourself remember. ... Remember what it is like to love and to be loved. Then open yourself to remembering what it truly means to love and be loved by the Goddess.

— Lazaris

It is no accident that during the culminating weekend workshops of November, 1993, we spoke about vortexes opening. Then we talked of the Vortex of the Archetypes, the Vortex of the Future, and of the Vortex of Sirius — the Vortex of the Goddess. For in 1994, the Sirius Vortex opened not just cyclically as it always does, and not just a little bit as it has always done. The Vortex of Sirius, the

Vortex of the Goddess, opened full and wide. And this event was played out in your heavens, there for all to see if you knew how to read the signs, how to read the celestial compasses.

Within your solar system, the opening of the Sirius Vortex was marked, its space held and its time measured, by the movements of one planet: Pluto.

Within your solar system, the opening of the Sirius Vortex was marked, its space held and its time measured, by the movements of one planet: Pluto.

Now when many of you think of this astrologically you think: "OK, Pluto. It gives out a specific kind of energy. Pluto does this or that. It causes …"

Understand: Your planets are vortexes, too. They are celestial gateways to other dimensions and, potentially, to other worlds. As vortexes, they hold space and time. They hold energy in formation — they hold information that can influence. Planets do not "do." They do not cause. You create your own reality, sometimes by causing and most often by allowing. You "do." You cause. Planets can influence with the energy that flows through them.

The dance of the planets — the movement of the planets in relationship to each other — can reveal the tracings of energy waxing and waning, ebbing and flowing, within your Solar System and in your Universe. In this way, a planet is like a compass. It can point the way to the flow of energy, but it does not cause that flow.

For example, a standard compass has a needle that is responsive to the flow of energy called magnetic north. The needle will always point north. By understanding the dance — by understanding the movement of this needle in relationship to magnetic north — you can find your way. The needle traces the flow of energy called magnetic north. It is not because the needle points in a certain direction that a location suddenly becomes north. The needle did not cause the direction to be north. It is because the direction is already north that the needle pointed in that direction.

The dance or the movements and relationships of the planets are as compass needles pointing in the directions of particular kinds of energy and, in so doing, abstractly tracing — marking and measuring — the flows of that energy.

The dance of Pluto did not cause the opening of the Vortex of Sirius. Pluto's dance pointed, marked, measured, and traced. It heralded a grand event. It heralded an event that had not happened in over 90,000 years. Pluto, compass-like, pointed the way. It held the space and marked the time.

The dance of Pluto: Now Pluto is called the Planet of Death. It is called the Planet of Regeneration. It is also called the Planet of New Birth and of New Life. It does not cause or produce these things; it does not "do" these things. Yet, Pluto does point, mark, measure, and trace the energy that allows such things to more readily happen or to more easily be created. It holds the space and marks the times when the possibilities and the potentials for such energies — the energies of death, regeneration, new birth, and new life — are most present and available.

So when one speaks of death and rebirth, of regeneration, or of new life — when one speaks of transmutation, transformation, transcendence — as being Pluto or as being what Pluto represents, what one is really saying is that this physical illusion called a planet is pointing, marking, measuring, and tracing the presence of a specific kind of energy with distinct possibilities and potentials of death, regeneration, rebirth, and new life. What is being said is that this physical illusion called a planet is holding the space and marking the time of possible transmutation and transformation and of potential transcendence.

Now, Pluto is a phenomenal planet in that it has the capacity, due to the shape of its elliptical orbit, of moving inside the orbit of its neighbor, Neptune. Normally, Neptune is closer to the Sun and thus to the Earth. Pluto, located beyond Neptune, is farther away from both the Sun and the Earth. But because of the shape of its orbit, Pluto does, upon certain cycling, move inside the orbit of Neptune, therefore moving closer to the Sun and to the Earth than Neptune.

In 1978 Pluto entered inside the orbit of Neptune, coming closer to the Earth than it had been in two and a half centuries. In 1978 its orbit moved inside the orbit of

Neptune. It was September 23rd, 1979, that we talked of the beginning of a New Age. It was no accident that we talked of it then, for when Pluto moved inside the orbit of Neptune, it pointed, marked, measured, and traced a time of death, of regeneration, of rebirth, of new life. It heralded what, for many, was the beginning of a New Spirituality.

Some people could only see the death aspect of it, but others could see the aspects of regeneration and rebirth, of new life. It is a time for transmutation, a time of transformation and transcendence — not that any other time is not, but this particular time is one of profound possibilities and potentials. Pluto moved within the orbit of Neptune in 1978. We began talking of a New Age and the New Spirituality on September 23, 1979.

Now Pluto stays inside the orbit of Neptune — at the closest point it has been in 250 years — until 1999, the end of this most monumental decade in history, the decade in which you will decide to create a future of dreams, to give birth to a Virgin Future, and to create a New World and a transcendent new life. Two magical decades, capped with the most monumental decade in history.

Now something else happened with Pluto. ...

From the vantage point of Earth, there is a huge circle called the Zodiac, 360 degrees of arc, divided into 12 segments of 30 degrees each. In 1984, not only was Pluto within the orbit of Neptune — closer to the Earth than it's been in 250 years — but also it moved into the arc segment of the Zodiac at 210 degrees, which is the Sign of Scorpio, the Eighth House.

Now Scorpio, for those who are not that familiar with astrology, is the symbol for and the representation of death, regeneration, rebirth, new life. It is the "house" of transformation, transmutation, and potentially of transcendence.

Pluto is now within its rulership in the Eighth House of the Zodiac. Such placement and alignment speaks to increased intensity of an already intense energy. The needle of the compass is not just pointing, it's quivering and it's flashing. ... {laughter} ...

Pluto entered 210 degrees and stayed in that 30 degrees of arc for ten years, moving into the 240-degree mark during 1994. For a decade from 1984 to 1994, it was within that arc, so intense in its energy of transcendence and transformation and transmutation — so intense in its pointing, marking, measuring and tracing of the energy of death, rebirth, regeneration and new life. Holding the space — within the orbit of Neptune and closer to the Earth than it had been in 250 years and within the House of its rulership — it suggested that something big could happen and would happen over those specific 10 years. And it did!

Now we look outside your solar system. Something else happened, and we look to the brightest star in your heavens. We look to Sirius.

Sirius is a star and a star system. As a star system, Sirius is composed of a bright star, called Sirius A, and around it, in an elliptical orbit — not a circular orbit, but an elliptical orbit —moves Sirius B, the dark star, the shadow star.

Now, because the orbit of Sirius B is elliptical, there is a certain time when Sirius A and Sirius B are the most separated from each other; there is a time when they are farthest apart. Likewise, there's a point when they are the closest together.

Sirius B has an orbit about Sirius A — a star about its star — that is 50.9 years. More easily said: 50+years. The movement of the Sirius system is such that during 1994, Sirius B moved into the position where it was closest to Sirius A. When Sirius A and Sirius B are the closest together — when they are "united" in wholeness, in completeness — it is called the Grand Union. During 1994, there was the Grand Union of Sirius.

So during 1994, there were two incredible astronomical and celestial occurrences. One can only happen every 250 years: Pluto, within the orbit of Neptune, within its rulership in the Eighth House or the House of Scorpio, is as close together with the Earth as it can be. The other can only happen every 50.9 years: the Grand Union of Sirius when Sirius A and Sirius B are as close to each other as they can be.

And on April 23, 1994, the Sirius system, 8.5 light years away, entered its Grand Union — and Pluto moved into exact alignment with it.

Such an astronomical and celestial event had not happened in more than 90,000 years; it could not have happened since then. And it will not happen again for another 90,000 years. The dance of Pluto pointed to, marked, measured, and traced a celebration of energy. As a compass, Pluto marked and measured the space and the time of a grand triumph for your Universe. When this rarest of rare alignments occurred, the Vortex of Sirius opened. The Vortex of the Goddess opened wide and full as it has not done in over 90,000 years.

The last time the Vortex opened, from the mists emerged a land, and upon the land a world stood out. There emerged Lemuria and a world of the mysteries and mysticism of the Goddess. In time, once its work was done and the seeds were scattered and planted through out the world, Lemuria would retreat into its mist and become the Land That Imagination Forgot. Yet it was out of the last Grand Opening of the Sirius Vortex over 90,000 years ago that the world of Lemuria began.

Yes, the Sirius Vortex — the Vortex of the Goddess through which all energy enters and leaves your Universe, through which all the Archetypal energy flows, through which your Higher Self's energy enters — opened wide and opened full. The Goddess blew a bubble of space and then filled that bubble with the fertile eggs and seeds of all growth.

This astronomical alignment — this celestial dance of planets and stars — can only happen every 90,000 years. It happened before; it happened again on April 23, 1994.

The Vortex opened full and wide, and there was a flood of Light — no, not light that you can physically see (light within the range from red to violet) — but with Light from the Imaginal Realm, from beyond the torus of space-time. That Light flooded into your Universe. And

Information — the Light Information or information carried on Light — flooded into your Universe.

On April 23rd, that flooding Light, that flooding Information, that flooding Light Information and Information Light, saturated the Earth and was absorbed. More specifically, it saturated you. The hologram of your brain absorbed the Light, absorbed the Information, absorbed the Light Information and the Information Light.

And you now have all the information you need to create a new world — all the information you need to make the choices that we all along said you would make. ... OK, we cheated. ... {laughter} ... You will choose a Future of Dreams for you, for those you love, for those you care about, and for your world — for your Earth. You will choose to give birth to a Virgin Future that has never been — that never could have been experienced before.

An analogy: We, and others, have suggested that your brain, in many ways, functions like a computer. Using that example, it is as if to say that on April 23rd, 1994, there was the most magnificent downloading ... {laughter} ... of the most magnificent program that there has ever been or that could ever be.

The Goddess is returning, and She brings with Her a Light, a Light that once lit cannot be extinguished. And your brain — that hologram that can function as a computer — now holds that program. It is not just within your brain; it is within everyone's brain. And it is within every cell of your body; it is within your DNA. It is within everyone's body and within everyone's DNA. Every human being, regardless of the station they assume they hold, received that downloading, that flood of Light and Information and that flood of Light Information and Information Light. It is within each and every one of you.

The Goddess is returning, and She brings with Her a Light, a Light that once lit cannot be extinguished.

But just as with a computer, how you use it, what you do with it, how you learn the program with what you now have within you, is up to you. It is up to you. There are people who have powerful computers, and all they use them for is to play games or as a calculator to balance their checkbooks. There is just so much there that they never, ever use.

On April 23rd, the Vortex of the Goddess, the Sirius Vortex, opened and flooded your Earth, flooded every cell of your body and every neuron of your brain with Light. Portions of your brain that have waited lifetimes — seeming to lie dormant or to function redundantly while waiting — are now filled and overflowing. Portions of your DNA also waited, ready to hold the information, ready to be awakened. DNA that is often called "DNA garbage" (because your scientists could not decipher the meaning) now holds the Light.

You see, you don't need extra strands of DNA. You've got plenty of room in the two you have, and they have absorbed this information.

The Opening of the Vortex was an event that had not happened in 90,000 years. And it was a day that outwardly looked no different than any other. It was not suddenly brighter. There was no great clash or calamity. For many it was to be an ordinary day. You see, it wasn't some "religious experience" in which the statues turned black or dark green ... {laughter} ... It was a downloading of information. The Goddess works quietly, gently.

It was a downloading of information that means that inside of you — inside every one of you — you have all that you need to create the New World that you've come to create. You have all you need to fulfill your destiny — to make the maps you came here to make, to dream your dreams and to weave them into manifested reality, to make visions, and to create realities. You have all you need to be the metaphysicians and the magicians that you yearn to be and have always been.

You have all you need to create the reality you want for yourself — with the rewarding friendships and intimate relationships — with meaningful and valuable work that celebrates your power, strength, and talent, and that expresses your value and dignity. You have all that you need to be successful and happy, to find triumph and joy.

There is help on the way ... Seriously and Siriusly. ... {laughter} ...

This is the time of death and of regeneration; it is a time of new birth and of new life. It is the time of the grandest transmutation, the grandest transformation, and, yes, of the grandest transcendence that has ever occurred. The Vortex of Sirius opened full and wide on one day in April, 1994. And everything is different now.

And you will spend the rest of your lives learning and coming to know, sorting and choosing, and using that Information, that Light, and that loving and healing.

This is why we have emphasized so strongly your becoming a receiver — a receptacle for the Light, a receiver. Yes, we talk of it in terms of receiving specific things, receiving for yourself, for those you love and for your world. We do not diminish such receiving.

But also, we have always meant it in the sense of the play upon words: Becoming this grand receiver of Her Light, becoming a grand receptacle of Her Love. That is why we have talked of the evolution of your computer-like brain, this hologram that is your brain. The areas of our emphasis with specific work with your temporal lobes, limbic brain, and hypothalamus (the governor of the brain) correspond to the cerebral areas that play a phenomenal role in the absorption, in the use, and in the distribution of this energy that is more than you can conceive, more than you can label.

Let it in: This is the energy that over 90,000 years ago produced an entire continent, a continent that came out of the mists and, in its time, would recede into the mists, becoming a Land That Imagination Forgot. Lemuria was literally there, though, as we have said for so many years, it will never be biologically, chemically, or scientifically proved. Lemuria was literally there; it still is. Even so, it exists beyond the Bridge of Belief and thus will never be captured and contained in the brittle prison of scientific proof.

This was the Vortex that opened and closed, never to be opened again until the Seals could be broken. Now, it has opened again, opening fully and completely. And it was a flood that penetrated to the core of your Earth — every rock, every blade of grass, every tree, every bit of mineral, plant, and animal life. And you, human being that you are, received it all.

Most will not know what they received and will never know in this life. But you can. That doesn't make you "better than" or special. It just means you are capable.

You are capable. You are the Mapmakers, the Dreamers, and the Dream Weavers. You are the Vision Makers. You are the Reality Creators. You are the Receivers. This is what you have been waiting for.

In the myriad of lifetimes that you've had, most of them began and ended, in your time-frame, between 80,000 years ago and a few decades ago. You have not had lifetimes where the Vortex of Sirius opened wide and full. In the scattering of lifetimes you call past, none of them landed within the fabric of your being that includes the previous Grand Opening of Sirius. It has now happened; it happened in one of your lifetimes. It happened in this one. It happened, and everything is different now. Practice is over, and everything is different now.

Through it flowed the Light and Love that can allow you to transcend what has been and to create what will be.

The worlds as we've talked of them — the potential worlds of nightmare, mediocrity, and dreams — have always been there. You could have chosen them at any time. Many have. Yet, those worlds have been far apart, seeming so separate from each other. Then they started coming closer, coming closer. Then in 1994, on April 23rd, a bridge: All the Light, all the Information, all the Light Information and Information Light to step into a New World became a part of you and your world.

When we speak of a New World, we are not talking about a New World Order. We are not talking of a political concept tossed about in your current world. The New World Order speaks to finding a new order to the existing or old world. That is not what we are talking about. When we speak of a New World, we mean a world that has never been. We mean a world that has never been.

The Vortex of the Goddess opened, and through it flowed a Light that will change, grow, transmute, and transform you. Through it flowed the Light and Love that can allow you to transcend what has been and to create what will be. And you are witness. You are participant. You are integral in this happening.

You are not alone, and you do not have to do it all by yourself. There is help. There is the Love and Light of the Goddess. You are not alone.

Resources

The following Lazaris tapes are helpful in working with some of the issues in this chapter or offer further exploration of related areas:

> *Letting More Love into Your Life*
>   *(This is a series of 12 tapes ... please see Appendix)*
> *Living Magically Every Day*
> *Cleaning Chakras / Pituitary-Pineal Meditation*
> *High Magic: The Ritual of Receiving*
> *The Double-Tetrahedron Technique & Meditation*

4

Allow Yourself:
Accessing the Light and Information

Techniques of Awakening
& Exploring

Life is a gift. Life is a gift from God/Goddess/All That Is given through the Goddess. Yours is to learn to receive. You are here to learn to elegantly and graciously receive that gift that life is.

Yours is to learn to receive. That's it. It's time.

— *Lazaris*

Please understand, now that the 23rd of April is past, it doesn't mean, "Well, that's it. I'm done." No. However well- or ill-prepared you were or assumed you were, you continue preparing, readying, and opening. You continue becoming and being the receptacle for the Light and for the Love. The Grand Opening of Sirius on that incredible date was not an all-or-nothing-at-all opportunity.

We would suggest that there are ways in which — particular techniques with which — you can work to augment this continuing and never-ending exploration. These ways, these techniques can also expand your current success and happiness. They can add dimension to your path and to your journey, depths to your power, and heights to your success.

This is the most monumental decade in the history of humankind. The Grand Opening of Sirius adds to the momentum of the moment; it expands the horizons and the vistas. With technique, you can develop the artistry and the mastery to add to your momentum of the moment and to expand your horizons and vistas of possibility and potential. The key is in the preparation.

How to prepare ...

We are going to suggest several ways. Because you are unique and individual, you will find that certain techniques work better for you than others do. Rather than saying, "This is it, take it or leave it," we offer several means toward the ends you seek.

1. Living Magically Every Day

First we refer to what's already been done.

There is a particular evening tape that is called *Living Magically Every Day.* Many of you have it among the pile of tapes that you have. Dig it out, because during that particular evening, we focused most particularly on how to run various energies: figure-eight energy, vertical energy, horizontal energy, scattered energy, and spiraling energy. We talked about how to work with these energies specifically in the morning and at various other times as well. Rather than saying, "Take a deep breath," and then continuing to describe the Energy Meditation, let us suggest that it is already on tape. It is already there waiting for you. Dig it out, those who have it, or it's available. But again, it is one technique among many. It's not as if you have got to do it, but it is available.

2. Pituitary-Pineal &
Beyond the Threshold Meditations

Another technique that is also recorded already for you is one that works with your pituitary and pineal glands — that works with your sixth and seventh *chakras* — which are also your personal etheric vortexes to higher realms. The particular audio cassette is called *Cleaning Chakras/Pituitary-Pineal Meditation*.

There are other meditations for these chakras, but this specific one is particularly powerful and can be profoundly useful in working with your Sirius Connection — in working with accessing the Light and Information that was downloaded into your universe, your world, and your body April 23, 1994.

Additionally, we suggest an audio cassette entitled *Beyond the Threshold/Editing the Film*. By moving beyond the threshold — your personal threshold of belief and imagination and your personal depth of self-trust and self-love — you can deepen and strengthen your preparation to receive. You can prepare your endocrine system, your electromagnetic field, your auric field, your etheric realm, and your energy patterns for that reception to come more elegantly and fully — and to be able to be used more quickly and easily.

3. The Teleportation Machine

Now a third approach that we suggest is to use the "Teleportation Machine" — the double-tetrahedron. *Tetra* means four, and *hedron* means sides. A tetrahedron is a four-sided geometric shape. All sides are triangular; there are three triangular sides and one triangular base. It is not a pyramid. A pyramid has five sides: 1, 2, 3, 4 triangular shapes plus a square or rectangular base.

A double-tetrahedron is created by joining the bases of two tetrahedrons. One tetrahedron points upward, and one points downward with the two bases joined as one. It looks like a diamond shape — a three-dimensional diamond shape. Each tetrahedron is the same size — as above, so below.

Pyramid

The tetrahedron is a Sacred Geometric shape. When doubled it can become a powerful device, a powerful machine, for teleportation and for so much more. When a tetrahedron spins clockwise or counter the clock, it creates a powerful force field of energy that can be released. When a double-tetrahedron spins, likewise, it generates a force field with unbelievable power. When that spinning double-tetrahedron also rotates top to bottom or bottom to top the force field and the power available can be dynamic, and it can be multidimensional.

If you are in the middle of this dynamic and multidimensional force field, the release of energy can be used to teleport you emotionally and mentally beyond space-time and to other places within space-time. With practice such a force field can be used to teleport you physically from one place to another. At first you will not teleport literally, but you can do it "really" on other levels.

Tetrahedron

This is a Teleportation Device. The secret of its success is that it is created in your imagination. It is not — we repeat, it is not — to be created physically. The secret lies within your ability to imagine it using your Living Imagination. Imagining.

This is the geometric device that was imagined in Lemuria by those who were known as the Crystal Climbers. Many of you, in your Lemurian lifetimes, were Crystal Climbers, and you used this Teleportation Device then. As you were called and then led into the Magic Land, you came upon the pillars — the huge pillars of sheer rock. The Crystal Cities sat upon these pillars, inaccessible except to those who could teleport to the top: Crystal Climbers. You used this device then; you can use it now.

Double-Tetrahedron

This is a Teleportation Device. The secret of its success is that it is created in your imagination.

This device has been used by those you call extraterrestrials. Dimensional beings from other planetary systems use such devices to fold space and to warp time. Multidimensional beings from other worlds also use such devices to appear in your world. Those dimensional and multidimensional beings do not have to rely upon linear travel at the speed of light or faster than the speed of light. They do not have to: They can use the Teleportation Machine — the one we describe to you here.

You see, there are vortexes — doorways and gateways — out there in your Universe and in the many universes other than your own. Stars and planets dot your heavens, and many are vortexes where energy enters your universe and where energy leaves your universe. The grandest of these vortexes is the Vortex of Sirius — the Vortex of the Goddess. And there are many others "less grand." Within certain stars and within certain planets, tetrahedron and double-tetrahedron energy waits. Such energy waits to be used to teleport.

Those that you call ET's can travel beyond the gravitational bounds of their planets just as your astronauts escape the bounds of Earth's gravity. They travel to one of these vortexes; they travel out to one of these double-tetrahedrons. They go inside. They spin, they rotate outside of space-time. Outside of time and beyond space. Then they re-enter time and space at a different location. From there they can travel — not at the speed of light, but with conventional speeds.

It is interesting to note that with the planets of your solar system there is tetrahedron energy. With the spin of the planets a powerful force field is created, and it releases immense energy into your universe. Your astronomers know, for example that the larger planets of your solar system give off more energy than they receive. They are not just reflecting the light of the sun, as it was once and until very recently assumed. They are giving off more than that amount of energy. The energy is coming from "inside" the planet. More truthfully, it is coming from "outside" your universe, through the vortexes that the planets, in fact, are.

There is tetrahedron energy within your Earth. Your Earth is creating a tremendous energy. Your Earth gives off more energy than it receives. Your sun gives off more energy than it should, according to the rigors of your science.

The energy is coming from "inside" the planet. More truthfully, it is coming from "outside" your Universe, through the vortexes that the planets, in fact, are.

As we have said, the planet Pluto does not make things die and be reborn, but is a vortex of the kind of energy that produces death, regeneration, and new life. As we also said before, Pluto points, marks, measures, and traces where such energy flows — waxing, waning, ebbing, and flowing — within your world. It is like a needle of a compass.

Jupiter is not a planet that causes benevolence and bounty. As a planet it is a huge vortex of energy emitting a phenomenal force field. Specifically there is a visible vortex of swirling energy located 19.5 degrees north of its equator. By the way, that 19.5 degrees is significant in the flow of tetrahedron energy and is repeated over and over again wherever tetrahedron energy is located. For example, with your Earth, with the sun, and with Jupiter, the tetrahedron energy is most concentrated at 19.5 degrees above or below the respective equators.

The stars and planets are vortexes. They are gateways of energy pouring into your universe. Those primitives who thought that heaven was like a fabric with all these tears in it, with all these holes in it, were righter than you know. … {laughter} …

The technique: Create this double-tetrahedron shape in your imagination — in your Living Imagination. Create it in your mind's eye, and make it big enough for you to get inside. You can create it in this more-real world of imagination to be solid or translucent; you can create it with open or opaque walls or transparent ones.

With the sides in place, you get in. Climb into this thing. Put your feet on two of the lower bars. Grab on for the ride of your life. Here you stand. … {laughter} … Did da Vinci do something like this? … {laughter} … Something about a golden mean, 3/5 and 2/5 or something like that. Such foolishness! … {laughter} …

There you stand, inside your double-tetrahedron, and you begin to spin. Slowly at first, then picking up speed, picking up speed until you are really spinning fast. Then spin faster still and still faster. This is what the Whirling Dervishes are trying to accomplish. Spinning, spinning,

spinning, spinning, spinning, spinning. Clockwise or counter the clock, spin.

Now once you are whirling around and around so fast that it seems as though you are "getting there before you left" — and here's the tricky part — start rotating. It is tricky and delicate, but with a bit of practice, you can continue the whirling clockwise or counter the clock spinning and begin to rotate top to bottom, bottom to top — forward or backwards.

And what is happening inside you? Do you have any idea the kind of chemicals that are being released? Do you have any idea the neuropeptides that are being pumped out? Do you have any idea of the neurotransmitters and neuroreceptors that are activated? Do you have any idea the way you are changing your brain, evolving your brain to receive? Do you realize what has to go on in the bloodstream, in the body system, what you're doing to every cell with just this "silly visualization" of spinning and rotating?

The pattern engages your mind and triggers massive electromagnetic energy — firings — in your brain. By using your imagination to spin faster and faster and faster until you are spinning in such a whirl — and then at the same time imagining the rotation combined with going faster and faster — you are using otherwise seemingly dormant or redundant portions of your brain. You are expanding brain function; you are expanding the hologram of the brain — and the hologram of reality that your brain can create.

Should we repeat that? With this pattern, you are using otherwise seemingly dormant or redundant portions of your brain. You are expanding your brain function, and you are engaging your mind to expand the hologram of the brain and the hologram of the reality that your brain can create.

And you see, so much more is happening. What ends up happening in this visualization is that within the more real realm (auric-etheric and imaginal), you break down to your molecular structure, to your atomic structure, and then into your subatomic structure.

Now, here's the kicker: You are spinning like nobody's business, and you are rotating, spinning and rotating, spinning and rotating. Within that imaginal, your body now dissolves. It is no longer this body with this coherence. It is incoherent now. It is totally disconnected. The molecular structure is broken down to the atoms. The atomic structure is broken down into subatomic particles. Your whole body is neutrinos and quarks and all of a sudden … whoosh! It has re-entered the nonlocality, and you are everywhere at once. You are everywhere at once. You are nowhere.

The truly important and the more profound teleportation is emotional and mental.

When you are ready, you can reconstitute yourself by imagining — by slowing down the spin and rotation, by stopping. From the nonlocal of nowhere, you can reconstitute yourself — collapse from the nonlocal wave function back into the very local particle function. With such collapse, you can reconstitute in a different space or a different place. At first it can be a different emotional-mental space. However, in time, it could also be in a different physical place.

The truly important and the more profound teleportation is emotional and mental. That is where you can begin. You can move beyond the maya of illusion and generate genuine change — emotional-mental change.

You see, while you are scattered, for example, you can leave your martyrhood, and come back — reconstitute — without it.

"Naaah!" … {laughter} … The birth of your first new belief: "Naaaaaaaah!" … {laughter} … And a brand new martyr is born, with a history already in place. … {laughter} …

"You mean I can spin and rotate and have no more martyr left?" In the nonlocality of it, you can leave your martyr out there. When you come back together again, you can be without it, and never have to be it again. We will let you extrapolate.

The exercise can take you outside of space-time. Some day in the future you may literally use it to teleport, meaning: You sit down, and you visualize your tetrahedron around you. You will start spinning and then rotating using your Living Imagination to access the imaginal of the Imaginal Realm. As well as imagining the disintegration of your physical body, it disappears. You reappear at some other location.

As we have already suggested, that is not the most important stuff. The important stuff is the emotional-mental stuff you leave out — leave behind — when you reconstitute. That's the real teleportation: from being one person to being another person. Location? You can get in a plane. It's just illusion. But going in as a martyr and coming out without it, going in this place and coming out a totally different person, now that's the teleportation that means something.

This exercise, even just doing it, just spinning and rotating without any intent of going anywhere, aligns you in such a way that it is a part of this preparation and continuation to receive the Light and the Information, to receive the Light Information and the Information Light, to receive the Light and Love of the Goddess.

4. Open-Ended Meditation

From time to time it is valuable to just do an open-ended meditation, where you sort of lie there and give yourself over to your Higher Self saying, "Do what you've got to do to me. Open my head. Do something. Do whatever you have to do so as to align, rearrange, redo, undo my body and my brain. Do what will benefit me the most right now to prepare and to continue my connection with Sirius and with the Goddess."

Perhaps it works best for you to say, "I give myself over for your loving and your healing." With this, do it. Open yourself to their love and healing in an open-ended meditation. Just let it happen. Just let it be.

We have often said that there is magic in the telling. With this technique — the fourth technique we mention — there is magic in the doing. There is more magic than you can yet know. Have fun exploring the possibilities and potentials that this technique can open up to you and for you.

5. Energy Visualization

On previous occasions we have talked about the influx of electromagnetic energy. This technique is built upon that phenomenon that is so prevalent in this most monumental decade and that will be increasingly prevalent in the new millennium with its positive future of dreams and its Virgin Future of magic and miracles.

For several years, we have talked of this increase in electromagnetic energy. Its purpose: to augment imagination, creativity, intuition, and wisdom. Each of these components is an essential building block of the positive future of dreams. The electromagnetic energy stimulates the temporal lobes and triggers electrical and chemical reactions within the cerebrum and within the limbic brain. Such stimulation also triggers new frequencies of vibration around the hypothalamus gland and within the intense concentration of neurotransmitters and neuroreceptors within the midbrain.

However, such energy needs to be utilized — consciously utilized. Unattended, this same electromagnetic energy can trigger tectonic activity — earthquakes and volcanoes. It can trigger seemingly attacking and unrelenting weather conditions — massive and excessive storms and bizarre weather conditions — as you have been experiencing over the last several years. Unattended, this electromagnetic activity can trigger emotional outbursts and violence. This, too, has been too evident and tragically painful in your current world.

This same electromagnetic energy that can be so helpful in your growing, changing, and evolving can also precipitate so much tragedy, sadness, and sorrow. And this energy is increasing as the years of this decade unfold. The influx increases and accelerates.

Technique: Imagine a beam of light coming down to touch your scalp. Sense it come through the skin, through the bone, into the brain, through the cerebral cortex, that 1/4" layer, through the cerebrum — that mousse-like substance — into the limbic brain, into the emotional center. Imagine this beam of light coming in through the top of your head into the limbic brain, and simultaneously arcing up and out in those two directions. Coming into the center of the brain, and then arcing, coming out the temporal lobes. Sense the energy coming in and then arcing out, simultaneously arcing out.

You can do this technique as desired to generate greater imagination, creativity, intuition, and wisdom. You can also use this technique when the electromagnetic energy is particularly high. Listen to the news. At times of heavy storms, tornadoes, hurricanes, horrific wind storms — or at times of unusual storms, excessive cold or excessive heat — use this technique to benefit yourself and to siphon off the excess energy and generate relief for those of your world.

During times of tectonic activity or at times of great social unrest, you can siphon off or funnel off this energy to the benefit of all. It is a phenomenally powerful way to work with the world around you and to add to your growth, change, and evolution.

Now a variation: Reverse it, so that there are two energies, one on either side, coming into the very root of your brain, coming in through your left and right temples, through your left and right temporal lobes, coming together, joining and bonding in the limbic brain — and then, in a moment, shooting out of the top of your head.

Now we must warn you, this technique is one way to get out of your body.

When it comes in through the top of your head, it arcs out gently in both directions. It is a gentle movement of energy. When you reverse it, it comes in through the sides of your head, coming to this point of convergence, and then shoots out of the top of your head very rapidly, very explosively.

Now we must warn you, this technique is one way to get out of your body. So sometimes when you shoot the energy out of the top of your head, your consciousness may go with it. OOBE: Out-of-body experience. ... {laughter} ... So don't be surprised if you are no longer in your body. You'll come back. You will come back. You may not always get out of your body, but if you do, you will always come back. You will come back, absolutely so.

Staying in your body or leaving it for awhile, the exercise works to continue your never-ending preparation, and it expands your imagination and creativity to work with the unfolding Light and Information. It expands your intuition and wisdom to work with the Light Information and the Information Light.

6. Hypothalamus Meditation

We want to suggest that the hypothalamus gland — the brain of your brain — is key to unfolding the "downloading" of all the Light and Information you need to fulfill your destiny and to create the New World. For those who may not know, the hypothalamus is a gland in the brain — within the limbic or midbrain. It is the governor of the brain as it is integral to all the functions of your brain and for the functioning of your brain and body together. A tiny gland, it is key. It is the gland that tells the energy where to go and what to do.

For purposes of meditation, you can visualize the hypothalamus as the size of a grape (it's actually a little smaller). Imagine it located in the middle of your brain. Your subconscious and unconscious know precisely where it is; you can imagine a less specific middle.

The limbic brain lies beneath the mushroom portion of the brain, and within the double-arched area known as the hypocampus. Between the two arches are the pituitary and pineal glands. There you will also find this grape-sized, elliptical gland that is the hypothalamus gland. As you have learned to exercise the pituitary and the pineal glands, so you need to work with exercising the hypothalamus.

Technique: Now the way you do this is when you first visualize the hypothalamus, visualize its surface as being a flat color with a matte finish. It is a color that is not reflective, a surface that is not shiny.

Begin exercising this gland. Maybe you squeeze it; perhaps you stretch it up and down or in one direction and then another. You could stretch it in several directions simultaneously. Once you have begun slowly, increase the speed of your imaginal activities. Go faster and faster. Stretching it up, up, up, up, up, down, down, down, down, down, left, left, left, left, left, right, right, right, right, right. Work it inside your head, faster, faster, faster.

And as you do this, you are going to notice it starts to get shiny. It is going to stretch, and it is going to become shinier and shinier until it looks like lacquer, until it's as shiny as Chinese lacquer — just wonderfully, brilliantly shiny. It looks almost wet. Work it and work it until you work up one drop, one drop secreted from the hypothalamus. And then let it enter your bloodstream. And that's all. It'll do the rest.

As you work it, all in your imagination, one drop secreted out of this now-shiny hypothalamus drops into the bloodstream, into the whole of the body. Magic can happen.

7. *The Beam of Light Technique*

Special Note: This is a technique you do only in your imagination. Do not do this technique with visible light.

The concluding technique that we suggest is to realize that your brain is hidden inside this cranium of yours, certainly so. But it also is hidden behind these two flaps of skin called eyelids. Your eyes are part of your brain. They are one of your grandest receivers of electromagnetic energy and of light, and thus they are one of your grandest receivers of information.

And so the last of the techniques is to imagine — and here again, using your imagination — that there is a source of light that is going to shoot a beam of light to your *mentally, mentally* open eyes. This source of light is going to shoot a beam of light — needle-sharp, razor-sharp, laser-sharp light — directly into your eyes. Fast, sharp, explosive, this beam drives directly into your pupils — first one beam into one eye, then a second beam into the other eye, blinding. The light blinds you. This is going to stimulate and alter the capacity of light your eyes can absorb.

Again we say it: Do not do this technique literally with a visual light. Do it only in your imagination. Do not do this technique literally.

But you see, your brain cannot distinguish between what you imagine and what you imagine … {laughter} … It cannot distinguish between the imagination that does its long division and the imagination that does not show its long division.

Here is a table (pointing at a physical table) showing its long division. You are imagining this table, and showing your long division.

Now over here is another table (pointing in the air) that you are imaging also, without showing your long division. But see, on this table (in the air) also … on this table you can see the bouquet of flowers that you can't see here (pointing to the literal table). … {laughter} …

One is with long division, one is without. And your brain cannot tell the difference between what you imagine and what you imagine, and it does not give a hang about the long division.

Now your body is imagined with long division, and it has a particular liking for other imagination that shows its long division, too. And it doesn't quite trust this imagination that does not show its long division. But your brain doesn't care. Your body cares. Your brain doesn't. Your mind — that which is beyond space-time and that is other than conscious — doesn't care, either.

So as you shoot the light, shoot the light, as far as your brain is concerned, it is all imagination, and it will change your capacity of seeing and absorbing the light. ...

~

Seven approaches. You don't have to do them all. Please hear us. You do not have to do them all. Let yourself pick and choose. Try this. Try that. This one ... whoa! Do the ones that went *whoa!* Work with them at your leisure and with your appropriate speed.

These techniques all work to align and to prepare you to become the literal receiver and many others to become the esoteric receivers of the Light and of the Information. We offer you these tools and techniques designed to harness the energy of the opening of the Vortex of the Goddess. We offer them with love and peace.

Journal Pages

... A place to explore our experiences ... a pause to allow them to be real; a place to discover insights born of experience ... a place to allow those insights to be real as well.

Living Magically Every Day

(After working with running the energy, it can be helpful to write about the physical shifts and changes that you experience. You may also want to write about the emotional and mental ones.)

Pituitary-Pineal Meditation

It can be helpful to write the thoughts and feelings that can precipitate into changes with the focus of thoughts and feelings into words.

Journal Pages

Open-Ended Meditation

Journal Pages

Energy Visualization

(You might want to chronicle times of funneling and the physical effect "out there" and the emotional and mental effect "in here".)

Journal Pages

Hypothalamus Meditation & Beam of Light Experience

Resources

The following Lazaris tapes are helpful in working with some of the issues in this chapter or offer further exploration of related areas:

Standing on the Verge: Elegant Visions Creating Magical Successes
The Powerful Secret of Reflection: "With Little or No Effort At All ..."
Utilizing Our Destiny: Consciously Directing Evolution
Explore the Wonder: A New Kind of Intimacy, a New Kind of Love
Creating Optimal Futures

5

The Sirius Connection

What It Can Mean in Your Daily Life

There are so many new beginnings, so many new changes, and so many opportunities to begin fresh. In so many ways, you can draw a line in the illusion, separating yourself from all that was. Come, discover new reasons to be and new opportunities to become. Come, let us show you such glorious surprises.

— *Lazaris*

Turn up your light. For even if you don't know where you are going, it will be brighter once you get there.

— *Lazaris*

The Grand Opening ... the Vortex of the Goddess ... the Vortex of Sirius ... There is magic in the telling. There is value in piecing together the story of Sirius. There is value in remembering the story. It is part of your heritage; it is part of your myth (lyrical ritual of growth and change). There is also value in being aware of what all this can mean here and now.

It is important to put the pieces together, and it is important to take the pieces apart. What specifically can you anticipate and expect now that the Vortex has opened full and wide? What changes will you experience in your world and in yourself?

You have a connection to Sirius. Sirius and its story are a part of who and what you are. What is that connection, and what does it mean in the days and nights of your life?

So we turn our attention to the specifics. We turn our attention to what to look for and what to expect now that the Vortex of Sirius is open and your Sirius Connection is active. Let us begin.

History Has Ended

History has ended. No, not the academic discipline, but the control of the past has ended. The Sirius Vortex — the Vortex of the Goddess — has opened. It has opened like it has not opened in over 90,000 years. With its opening, you now have all the Information and all the Light necessary to evolve the human species, to trigger the metamorphosis of the human species. And even more, you have all you need to create a New World — not just a new order to an old world, but a New World — in which a new kind of human being can participate and thrive. Yes, the Vortex has opened wide and full. And everything is different now.

As we have said before, so we remind you: Practice is over. Now everything counts, everything matters. All your thoughts, all your feelings matter like they never have before. You cannot "practice" your metaphysics and your spirituality anymore. Now it is time to live it. Everything is different now.

What does it mean, day in and day out? What does it mean in the nuts and bolts of your reality?

Part of what it means is that you can no longer play patty-cake with your martyr or hopscotch with your negative ego. You can no longer play the flirtatious game of "maybe I'll give you up and maybe I won't." Your negative ego and the dark sides of self are playing for keeps now. They are hitting, and they are hitting hard. Those aspects of self can "cheat." Your martyr, your self-pity, and your negative ego do not always "follow the rules." Though reality is an illusion, it is a very serious illusion that suddenly became more serious.

You cannot play. Many of you hear that and think, "Yeah, yeah, yeah." And then you find out … "Oh, it's really true" … because you can get hit, and you can get hit hard.

In the seminar on Ecstasy we talked of the entanglements, the problems, the crises, and even the tragedies that are current in your reality. Because practice is over, whatever your personal entanglements, problems, crises, even tragedies may be, now they matter more, now they count more. They cannot be left on the back burner. Your entanglements, projections, games, problems, crises, and tragedies can — not will absolutely, but can — become more intense. We say these things not to scare you, but to alert you.

As the past relinquishes its control, the influence of the future expands. However, there is a "pipeline" of futures that you may not even realize you have. Through the years, you may have inadvertently created a full range of futures of which you are not currently aware. Some of those futures could be quite dark, extremely dark.

Futures, light or dark, are created by your thoughts and your feelings. They are created by your attention and by your intention, which, respectively, manifest and order your reality. Some of those futures that your thoughts, feelings, attentions, and intentions created long ago might otherwise lie dormant. They might never have become manifest in the three dimensions of space and one of time that you call your reality.

Now, because practice is over and history has ended, those otherwise dormant futures — yes, your potential light futures — could manifest with tremendous impact. And those otherwise dormant futures, your potential dark futures, could manifest with devastating impact as well. Devastating impact on you.

The growth that you have been "meaning to get to when you have time" and the growth that you have been consciously or unconsciously procrastinating can come up and slap you right in the face, right in the reality, very hard. Responsibilities you ignored, or erroneously thought you didn't have to take or could just dismiss, can come up and haunt you. It can be pretty frightening that practice is over.

But it also can be incredibly, incredibly beautiful. "Past has ended" and "practice is over" can mean you can be totally free from that personal past. It can be a genuine freedom. It can mean that you can stop playing the games: Get off the game board with your negative ego. Stop the game or the dance with your martyr. It is over. It is done. An ended past and a concluded practice can mean that you can get to the root of those entanglements, and you can undo them in the future before they fully manifest, before they become more intense.

You see, maybe you have not allowed yourself to really change the past. Many of you believe that you can work with the past, that you can compensate for it, or that you can even overcome your past. However, change it? Certainly you can, but so many of you do not believe that you can. "It's not allowed" in your belief system. After all, you convince yourself, "The past has already happened. It is a matter of record, right? Work, compensate, overcome, but you cannot change it." Regardless of rhetoric, most believe they cannot change the past, not really.

But you do believe you can change the future. Therefore, the entanglements, problems, crises, and tragedies already in progress are things you can intercept and change.

Yet when you change the future, you change the present. It has always been true: The future creates the present and lays it against the backdrop of the past. Now it is becoming truer than it has ever been. When you change the future, you change the present: Your entanglements can change. Sometimes they can change right before your very eyes.

You can play catch-up now — not by working extra hard, not by burning the candle at both ends, but by changing the future. By owning a current painful or fearful reality, you can scan the future to see where the current pain or the current fear could lead. In other words, you can discover the future that is creating the present — the future that is creating the current pain or the current fear. Once discovered, you can work with specific and precise technique to "disconnect" the dark future. Then you can use this "disconnected power" to actually and literally create a different future — to create a brilliant future — that can create a different present.

Yes, as incredible as it may sound to some of you, the current reality of pain or fear can change. It can dramatically change. What used to be considered a fanciful experience can now work in ways that can startle you, that can amaze you. Everything is different now.

You can empty the pipeline. You can clear out discordant realities and fill that pipeline with unbelievably positive, powerful, beautiful futures. You can create what we call Optimal Futures — futures that may not in any logic be able to manifest for decades to come, but from which you can benefit now.

Those of you in your thirties can create the future of what it's going to be like when you're eighty. What kind of world are you going to have when you're eighty? What kind of peace? What kind of spiritual awareness? What kind of wisdom? What kind of physical well-being are you going to have at eighty?

And even though it may be half a century before you are there, that future that you create can alter your health now. It can alter choice and decision before you even know that choice and decision are connected to that future. You can create Optimal Futures that will not be yours for decades, but which will alter your decisions and choices, your thoughts and feelings, today. Those Optimal Futures

You can create Optimal Futures that will not be yours for decades, but which will alter your decisions and choices, your thoughts and feelings, today.

can create current success and present-day happiness. Yes, they can.

The Evolution of the Human Species

When we talk of an evolution of the human species, we are not talking figuratively. We are talking very, very literally. Just as you have a prehensile thumb, just as you stand erect (which was a process not of linear evolution but of exponential or consciously-designed evolution), there is change occurring in your very physiology, in your very brain, and in the very function and the very shape of certain portions of that brain.

There is very literally an evolution taking place, and there is the positive future that will prevail for everyone who's willing to step into it, back into it, fall into it, or end up in it by default. ... {laughter} ... It just won't be there for those who intentionally choose not to be there, and that is their choice.

And there is a New World. You see, as we have said for so long, there really is no "solution" to certain problems that you have in your linear world. So you need to create a new world — not by scrapping the one you are in, and not by "fixing" it, but by changing it. Though indeed much of what you do may look like the dance called "fixing it," in fact, that dance will be creating the resonance, the space, of change. So often we have said it: It is not about fixing, it is about changing. It is not about curing, it is about healing. That truth has suddenly become truer.

This human evolution, this evolution of the human species itself, is more correctly a metamorphosis. It involves the emergence of a new kind of human being. This change is essential to creating a New World. Your brain is a hologram that projects holographic images of body and of world. In order to project a New World, you need an evolved cranial hologram. That is what this evolution, this metamorphosis, is about.

The new kind of human being will have a new kind of brain that can literally sense the New World. We mean it very literally when we talk of Virgin Futures, of positive futures of dreams, of an evolving human species. We mean it more literally than you currently can believe — than you can currently imagine.

Intention

First of all, when the Vortex opened wide and full, when your entire Universe was flooded with all the Information and Light, it was also flooded with an energy of acceleration. As a result, intention becomes much more powerful now.

Intention is what orders and prioritizes your reality. It is what orders and prioritizes your consciousness. You have conscious awareness. Some of it you call memory. Some of it you call fantasy. And there are varying degrees of consciousness about all kinds of things in this patch-work reality that is your current life. That consciousness with its varying degrees also bleeds through into the larg-er, more esoteric holographic Fabric of Being — into the holograms that you call past lifetimes — that is you and that which you call yours.

You see, you tend to say this life you are currently experiencing is your lifetime. More correctly, all your life-times are part of your Fabric of Being. The current lifetime is the portion of that Fabric that you are experiencing now. But it is all happening simultaneously, and it is all part of your consciousness. And it is your intention that gives order to the otherwise chaotic, fragmented pieces of your consciousness. Intention — your intention — is what arranges the pieces.

It is estimated by your scientists that you have 50,000 thoughts a day. 50,000 thoughts. Write them down. ... {laughter} ... The first 20,000 are "I don't know, I don't know, I don't know." ... {laughter} ...

You have 50,000 thoughts a day, and each of those thoughts has a feeling connected to it. It is your intention that sorts and orders them, connects this one and that one, and this one and that one. Intention gives order to the chaos and creates what you later will call logic and reason. So many dismiss intention. Only when it becomes their personal logic and reason does it become absolute.

Intent is increasing in importance now. Due to the influx of energy, intent is becoming more and more powerful. However, that increase is nonlinear. Intent is stretching higher, but it is also sinking lower. This means that instinct, which is at the core of your intent, will either degenerate into primal biology and chemistry — into more animal-like nature — or it will elevate into personal character and spiritual character that will supersede and override the seemingly unconscious chemical, biological, animal response that is in you. It will descend, or it will rise to respond instinctively to a more Real Self — to respond more to who you are becoming than to who you have been.

Second, it means that your needs will either degenerate or rise. Your needs — which are for survival, security, a sense of belonging, self-esteem, creating and producing, knowing, and aesthetics (your very spirituality) — are part of your intent. You will find people more and more focused on the base needs of survival and security: "Me, mine, what I need, what I've got, taking care of my own, taking care of myself."

In your world — with the amount of disease that is airborne, with the amount of disease that is nonresponsive to the allopathic traditions — in many ways it becomes frightening to go out there into the world. And many people will retreat into their survival mode, into their security mode. Their needs will reach toward the low end as opposed to lifting to the higher end.

Yet it is also true that because intent is so much more intense, many of you are going to find that your needs have been met, and that you can stretch even higher by turning your intention to your preferences. Your intention is so much more acute, so much more powerful now that it is altering your instinct — it is altering your needs.

Third, it is altering your drives. In some people drives such as genetic/hormonal drives, social drives, negative

ego drives, and personality drives will descend into obsession. On the dark side, you will see people in your world
approaching things from a more manic/depressive-like
energy. You will see greater frenzy and an increase in what
seems to be an almost insane focus: obsession.

However, on the light and lighter side, these and other
drives will move toward integration. There will be a
"drive" toward grace, toward elegance, toward embracing
a certain panache and aplomb. You will see intention turn
into manifestation without a whole lot of work going on in
between.

The fourth component of intention is desire. Desire
became part of your intention when choice became part of
the complexity of your life. Desire complicates things at
times. Nonetheless, it is part of your intention. Now, with
the Vortex opening, desire can ebb to its lower levels:
greed, self-centeredness, self-absorption, and self-obses-
sion. Sadly, you will see the ebb of desire in the lost eyes
and the empty countenance of so many. You will see it and
feel it in the "whatever" attitude adopted by so many.
(Whatever attitude: nothing matters, nothing is more
important than anything else ... whatever).

Even so, you will also notice a new flow of desire as
well: A new and refreshing flow of desire that has not yet
been imprisoned by consensus words and definitions will
break the surface of reality. This flow with no name or
description, this effervescent desire, can lift and change
people. It can ignite a passion for life and for living. Yes, it
can.

Because intention has become so much more acute and
so much more powerful, instinct, need, drive, and desire
— whenever and wherever they are focused now — will
intensify. If they are headed in the downward direction,
they will plummet. And you will look and say, "Wow, this
is the Goddess?" No. "This is what comes when the Vortex
opens?" No. This is what happens when more acute and
more powerful intention plummets to the depths of darkness or when it is allowed to follow the descent of entropy.

Be conscious. By being conscious you can reverse the descent. You can lift your instinct up into a strength of character with intuition; you can lift base needs higher, and needs met to the wondrous level of preference. Drives can be consciously directed to reach heights of grace and elegance. Desire can wax to its heights where you desire for yourself, but also for something beyond you, something bigger than you.

Attention

What other changes will there be? You will experience an increase in the importance and in the impact of attention.

Now attention is what defines and thus determines what is "conscious" in your consciousness. Attention defines what you manifest in your illusion. So often we have said this: What you pay attention to is what you create. If you spend your days feeling sorry for yourself, and spend one hour releasing self-pity, do not be surprised if you have self-pity in your life. "But I did the meditation. I did it three times. I listened to the tape, and I took real good notes."

Yes, and that's valuable, certainly so. And probably you were not feeling sorry for yourself in the midst of your processing and programming. But if you go right back into self-pity as soon as you put down your pen and paper, then your attention is on self-pity. And what you pay attention to is how you select the reality that is conscious to you.

You see, it's all out there: Everything from the very worst future to the very best — everything from instant death to longevity — is available to you. Where you put your attention is what determines what becomes conscious and what happens in your reality. Attention — with its intricacy of thinking, feeling, imagining, and expecting — is unbelievably more acute, more intense, and more powerful since the Opening of the Vortex.

People who are locked into downward spiral thinking — "it's going to be bad, it's going to be terrible, the end times are coming" — are going to select from among the possibilities the realities that look more and more like nightmares and mediocrity. Those who hold their feelings in the negative range, refusing to lift and change their attention, will select those realities that most reflect and most motivate negative feelings. What you pay attention to becomes more important than ever.

Likewise, what you imagine and what you expect are more important than ever. That's why we talked this year of expectation, its mystery and magic, and the importance not just of pumping it up, but of giving it substance that has genuine height, width, and depth. What you expect, with little or no other technique attached, with very little other thought, is going to more quickly start manifesting in your reality.

"Well, gee, I just kind of gave it a ... whhhhht! ... and there it was!" ... {laughter} ... Attention is now like a dull knife that suddenly became sharp.

For example, when you are thinking and feeling about something in your past, you can shift your attention, and you can be done with it. The only caveat is: Make sure that you have removed the gifts and treasures from that past. Make sure that you have taken back the power that you have hidden there. That's why we have talked so much about taking back the power that you lost in the unfinished pieces of the past. You see, even though the past is over, even though its control is released, because you pay attention to it, because you think it, because you feel it, because you expect it, because you imagine it, you keep living it. You keep it alive with your attention and with your intention.

So why don't you just forget it? What a wonderful therapeutic technique that is: Just forget it. ... {laughter} ... "You know, before I remembered it, I did forget it!" Right? ... {laughter} ... "I didn't have any recall. I was better off."

No, you were not. Why not? Because there were treasures and gifts inside that past. Because there were things that you needed to learn in that past. Therefore, you would not let it go. And "just not thinking of it" was not enough.

It was there in the unexpressed or the nonactualized feelings in the Unconscious Mind. Then you brought it from the Unconscious to the Conscious when you were strong enough, when you were capable of handling it.

And who brought it? Your Soul. "Well, thanks a whole heap." … {laughter} … Exactly. Because your Soul knows: You have got to deal with this. You have got to deal with the pain. You have got to deal with the shame. You cannot just shove it into the Unconscious, because you are still thinking it, and you're still feeling it, you just are not admitting it. And you are still expecting it even though you are not fully conscious of it.

Why? Because you put it in your Unconscious. The expectation is still there, and you are still imagining it even though it's not conscious. Perhaps you have dreams of being suffocated, of being hurt, of being somehow violated. Maybe you have fantasies, you have fears when someone gets too close to you.

You see, you are still imagining, you are still expecting, you are still thinking, you are still feeling. The attention is still there, but it's in the Unconscious. When you are ready, your Soul brings it into your consciousness. Then you need to pay attention to it so you can process it, so you can understand it, so you can sort it out and lift the attention which has held it in place. Learn the lessons that you need to learn, that you decided to learn.

No, you did not choose to have that tragedy, that horror in your life, but you chose to learn the lesson that the tragedy or horror represents. That was your intent. That was why you linked those pieces of consciousness together: to meet some instinct, some need, some drive, some desire. And you gave it attention to keep it in your reality. If you will learn the lessons, you can release it.

Many of you have learned so much. Maybe you have learned enough of that lesson. "Why won't it go away?" Because you have not extracted the gifts, you have not extracted the treasures.

Maybe you have. Maybe you honestly have extracted all the gifts and treasures and have learned all the lessons from the created reality. Then the question arises, "What more could there possibly be here?" When you are right, when there is nothing more to be gleaned or to be learned, you ask, "Why won't it go away?" Your attention. Drop it from your attention, and it will cease. It will.

"You mean I can … " Yes. "Don't I have to process it some more?" … {laughter} … "Isn't there some technique?"

Yes: Choose. … {laughter} … Just drop it.

"OK. I want to make sure it went away." … {laughter} …

You're paying attention. That's why it's following you. … {laughter} …

"It's still following me." … {laughter} … "OK, I will not pay attention. I will not pay attention to the shame and the hurt and the molestation I had as a child. I won't pay attention." … {laughter}

Pink elephants, right? … {laughter} …

Please understand: Because the Vortex opened — because intention and attention are more intense, because everything is different now — you can drop the past. If you have taken the treasures and gifts, if you have taken back the power that was left there, then you can drop the attention and be done with it. And you can turn your attention to other thoughts and other feelings, other expectations, other imaginings, and it will be different. It will be different.

Resources

The following Lazaris tapes are helpful in working with some of the issues in this chapter or offer further exploration of related areas:

Healing Ourselves and Our World with Resonance
The Mysterious Power of Chakras
Renewing Chakras
New Maps to More Elegant Futures

6

The Sirius Connection

More of What It Can Mean ...

Conjuring things that have never been and walking among them, touching, feeling, and responding: Imagining allows you to fancifully sail into the future to explore and bring back the gems — the thoughts, feelings, ideas, and concepts — that are waiting there, that are waiting there just for you. Remember: Always imagine. Always imagine, and always cherish your ability to do so.

— Lazaris

... The yearning is so deep and so much a part of who you are. You will do whatever is necessary to respond to the hunger, to the thirst for God/Goddess/All That Is. You will use whatever avenues are available — available to you.

— Lazaris

The past has relinquished its controlling and suffocating grip, and the future ever increases its influence. Your past has ended its imprisoning hold, and you can be free.

And a world is evolving: A species — your human species — is evolving. And amid it all, intention and attention, which have so often been assumed or ignored, rise or loom upon the many personal horizons you call the future.

Yet with your Sirius Connection, you are not alone. There is help, and you can receive that help. You have all the Light and Information you need. So let us continue. What more can it mean in your daily life?

Resonant & Impact Causation

Ultimately, all causation is resonant causation. There is only a sliver of reality that responds to colliding or impact causation. And for the several hundred years, you have chosen — individually and collectively — to live within that sliver to make it appear as though causation is only mechanical (Newtonian or classical mechanics) and that it is a linear process of collision, conflict, conquering. You have wanted to hold causation as mechanical and as a linear process called cause and effect. You have chosen to make it appear as if causation is a comparative and competitive process of the survival of the strongest, the fittest, the most intimidating, overpowering, and dominating influence.

Now that history has ended and everything is different, resonant causation, which has always been the ultimate causation of everything, becomes more and more intense, more and more evident, more and more visible, while impact causation becomes weaker and weaker and weaker.

Now that is going to make a lot of people really angry. They are not going to like this shift in paradigm, and they are not going to want to accept it. Perhaps the angriest and thus the most resistant will be the male chauvinists, regardless of their gender, who are counting on a system of reductionist logic, a system of linear evolution, a system of conflict, a system of impact, and a system of cause leading to effect.

And they are relying on it because that is what the whole system of singular authority and male dominance is based upon: that men are better-than because they can have more collision impact. They can compete and conquer. The thinking goes, "Men are stronger, they are faster

... if they're in condition. ... {laughter} ... If they are not in condition, well ...it's not fair. ... {laughter} ... They are still better than others." Or so you are told, so you are conditioned to believe.

As the paradigm of causation shifts, the chauvinist in you is going to rebel. Therefore, the inner chauvinist in you is going to "show up" in your world. You will experience more and more people trying to prove that cause and effect is real with impact that is more harsh, more punishing, more filled with conflict and with competition.

You see Korea, Bosnia, the Middle East, Los Angeles, Haiti, Africa, places erupting with harsh, colliding, and destructive impact. People are calling for strong-impact action. We are not suggesting one politics or another. Beyond the particular politics, it is clear that you are creating (causing or allowing) a reality in which "once again we have to use force in this way."

It is as though you are trying to reinforce the doctrine of cause and effect. Though the range of reasons why is complex, one of those reasons is an attempt to hold the old paradigm together. The current and ongoing increase in violence and dominance is a sort of last throes, if you will, of a dying paradigm. Reality is changing now. Resonant causation is replacing mechanical causation. Resonance is becoming stronger.

Because of resonant causation, dreams and dreaming are becoming more potent, more powerful. You can begin to generate a reality in which you can dream a different world. You can dream people being different. Perhaps it will begin with night dreams and then spread to daydreams, to conscious dreams, to conscious visions, and to meditations. The new dreams can extend to a new kind of intuition, a new kind of gestalt, and to any number of new ways of dreaming.

The Lemurian Dreamer Technique of "it's a dream, it's a dream, it's a dream" is going to work for some of you as it has never quite worked before. Aaaah! ... {laughter} ...

The Lemurian Dreamer Technique of "it's a dream, it's a dream, it's a dream" is going to work for some of you as it has never quite worked before. Aaaah! … {laughter} …

"You mean I can change the reality by touching my finger here and there and saying a few words and then dream what I want and I will get it? It will happen? I don't have to go out there and manipulate? I don't have to go out there and cajole? I don't have to go out there and try to make people feel guilty? I don't have to go out there and whine and cry and beg and …" … {laughter} … "Well, that sounds like anarchy!" … {laughter} … "We can't have people doing that!"

Fear can arise … "What are you dreaming about me? What are you dreaming about me?" … {laughter} … "Don't you dream me different!" … {laughter} … "What if everybody went about dreaming everybody else different? There would be chaos; it would be anarchy!"

But it does not stand alone, does it? Intention. Attention. Resonance. They all work together. And your Soul is more involved than ever. Your Soul is not going to let you dream someone robbing a bank so they will get put in jail. … {laughter} …

"Well, what if I'm not in touch with my Soul?" Then you are not going to allow Resonant Causation to work as elegantly or as effectively as those who are in touch with their Soul. It is something of a positive catch-22, isn't it? There are some unscrupulous people out there who might want to dream "bad dreams" for other people, but they do not know anything about their Soul, so a dreaming technique will not work for them with any elegance or with any ease.

The requisite is: That level of spirituality where you will allow it to work with excellence is the same level of spirituality where you have the spiritual character to hold and use the proper intent, attention, and resonance. You will have the appropriate spiritual character.

Further, it is not so much about dreaming other people to be different as it is about dreaming yourself to be different, about dreaming the future and the resonance of that future. It is about shifting your thoughts, shifting your feelings, shifting the attention and intention to create a different resonance that will open you up to a whole new range of futures. As we have said before: Whatever your resonance, there is a unique wedge of possible futures that can survive within that resonance. There are certain dark and light futures, and the higher that resonance is, the less dark the darkness and the brighter the brightness. The lower that resonance is, the darker the darkness and the dimmer the brightness.

If your resonance is low, perhaps the most positive future you can create is Nothing Going Wrong. … {laughter} … But not everybody is there. If someone's resonance is higher, then Nothing Going Wrong may be their mid-range, and all kinds of success lies in their top range.

Illnesses have their own resonances. Therefore, within a certain frequency there are certain diseases that do not exist — cannot exist. No matter how contagious they might be in another resonance, they do not exist here.

We are not saying it's OK to step out in front of a bus because it is not in the radiance of your resonance that you will be hit by a bus. You see, you can tell yourself that you can step out in front of a bus because it is "not possible that I'll get run over by a bus," but as soon as you start contemplating it, paying attention to it, your resonance starts to change. And by the time you reach the curb … {laughter} … you have shifted resonance. Now you step out in front of the bus, and you get smashed. And your dying words are, "But, but, but … it wasn't supposed to be there." Neither were you. … {laughter} …

How do you hold and lift resonance? By working with the Seven C's: Centering, Clarity, Choice, Commitment, Complexity, Challenge, and Creativity. Commitment — there in the middle of the list, the fourth C — is a resonance holder and lifter. The authenticity, the clarity, the courage, the perseverance, the conviction, the coherence, and the acceptance that are inherent in commitment hold resonance. They also lift it.

Complexity means to differentiate and integrate simultaneously. To seek complexity is to look for the individuality and the uniqueness of you.

Complexity means to differentiate and integrate simultaneously. To seek complexity is to look for the individuality and the uniqueness of you. And simultaneously, it is also blending that uniqueness — that difference —

with the Oneness and the beauty of that Oneness. To be separate and autonomous, and yet at the same moment to be One, is complexity. Challenge, creativity ... centering, clarity, choice ... All are part of holding resonance.

With the opening of Sirius, resonant causation — the ultimate causation — becomes now more visible, more apparent, more powerful.

Spiritual Hunger

On a very personal, very private level, understand that when the Vortex opened, it filled you with the Light, and that Light is now inside you and everyone else. Therefore, what you are going to notice in your world is that everybody is going to be reaching for their own spirituality — not for your spirituality, mind you, but for their spirituality. It is not that others will copy you or will begin doing your spirituality. Nor is it as if everybody is going to start reading spiritual books, meditating, and talking metaphysics. People will find their own ways, and those may involve ways quite different from your own.

And with the Light, with that energy now inside of all of you, people are going to respond to that hunger, perhaps without even knowing why. They are going to respond to a thirst that they perhaps don't even understand.

There are so many ways to respond to this spiritual hunger — to this spiritual thirst. For example:

1) People will seek human dignity for themselves, for those they love, for those they care about, and for all of humankind. Human dignity is integral to the spiritual quest.

2) They will seek to allow the Unconscious to become Conscious with a certain ease and a certain elegance. The Unconscious Mind has always released information into the Conscious Mind. Too often such release is accompanied by crises of loneliness or pain. The spiritual quest yearns for new ways to allow the emergence of the Unconscious into the Conscious.

3) Further, people will reach for a sense of longevity and immortality. People will give greater attention to things eternal.

4) Additionally, they will search for a deeper sense of goodness and truth.

5) They will yearn for the blossom of desire and expectation — for the blossom of imagination.

Beauty or violence. In your world, people will either reach for more beauty, or they will reach for more violence.

These qualities, these answers, can be found in the pursuit of beauty. Clandestinely, they can be found in the depths of violence. Ironic, but true. Those who commit hideously violent acts often talk of human dignity and unconscious truths finally revealed. They often speak of immortality and eternity. They are often convinced their violence has purpose and meaning: to vindicate goodness and truth. Though it seems insane to most, those who commit such violence often feel content: Their desires, though not the ones of their victims, have blossomed. Yes, the spiritual hunger can be answered, for some, in violence. Though the end results and the form are totally different, the function of beauty and the function of violence can be the same.

Beauty or violence. In your world, people will either reach for more beauty, or they will reach for more violence. The Goddess is returning, and the battering of women is increasing. Rape is increasing. How can this contradiction of violence and beauty be? As the true feminine energy emerges, some will embrace it, and some will attack it. Both are trying to answer a hunger and a thirst. This is not so say that violence is OK, nor that one should look the other way. No. But understand: You will have greater violence or greater beauty.

And there are other dichotomies:

Love or pain. We have talked of it before. The way to know someone, truly know someone, is to either love them or to inflict pain upon them. To truly be loved or truly be in pain is the way to know someone or to be known.

Enchantment or Crisis. In the depth of crisis there can be incredible growth. At the April, 1994, Los Angeles Intensive we talked with a woman. Four years ago, she faced her "terminal" cancer and her terrible home situation. She faced the fact that her whole life had fallen (was not just falling) apart. She faced all this four years ago because that was when her husband, in financial ruin, committed suicide. Massive crisis. Now, many years later, she speaks of it as the most unbelievable time of growth, the most enchanted experience. For in the depth of crisis, some — not everyone, but some — will answer that hunger, answer that thirst.

Designed Solitude or Chaotic Loneliness. Here again, we do not say it is a good way, but understand that is why some of you are so unbelievably lonely — not just alone. You are desperately responding to a hunger and a thirst. Solitude, designed solitude, would work more beautifully and more positively.

You are going to see in your world those who understand and seek beauty more consciously and those who seek violence more consciously. Those who seek love and those who seek pain. Those who seek enchantment and those who seek crisis. Those who seek solitude and those who sink into loneliness. The Vortex opened and filled you with all the Light and all the Information. It also has awakened a hunger, awakened that thirst, more deeply in each of you. And even for those who have no idea what we are talking about, that thirst and hunger is there. Expanding.

You are going to see it in your world. And depending on your intention and your attention and where you slide your resonance, you will see it in your reality. You will see it in your reality.

And so be aware of it and work within yourself, because everybody is going to respond. Your world is going to become much more spiritually aware. Whatever vocabulary, whatever vernacular, is used, it is going to be there more and more, everywhere. And you are going to feel a little vindication. ... "Um, hmm, hmm." OK, feel it a little bit, and get off it ... {laughter} ... and just rejoice and keep stretching, responding to your hunger, to your thirst.

Chakras

Just as the Vortex of the Goddess opened, so each of your vortexes — your *chakras* — has been changed.

Your first *chakra* of security is now functioning at a different frequency than it used to, and issues of security and the manners and means of creating it — physically, emotionally, mentally, etherically — are going to change. Now maybe you have not become aware of it yet, but your *chakras* are functioning at a different frequency.

It's almost as if the dial on the resonance of each chakra has been changed, as though the settings on this radionic device that is your body have been recalibrated. Therefore, you can expect to feel changes in each of these arenas — particularly the physical *chakras*. You are going to find yourself feeling and thinking and expressing differently.

Some of you may, others of you may not, like the sensation. New is not always comfortable. Certain of the recalibrations may have countered, in a way, certain other more familiar calibrations. Imbalances may occur. Your *chakras* are very loose, very fluid right now. Some of them have been "locked in and locked down" for years. Maybe longer. You know, the old combination lock has not been turned in years ... {laughter} ... rusted. Change is not always comfortable: "This is my frequency, and that's it."

Well, the ball bearings have been greased, and what it is going to mean is that you need to be more aware: "What is my intent here? What is my attention? What resonance do I want to set?"

Now you can be more conscious in adjusting your own *chakras*. If you are in a reality where your physical security is being threatened, you can change that frequency. If you are feeling stuck and blocked in primal creativity energies, you can change that frequency. If you are being too vulnerable at the moment, you can dial it down. You can open up to more love, and to a greater sense of intuition, knowing, psychic awareness, and psychic energy. And you can adjust your connection with your Higher Self to have it be closer. And all of this you can do more consciously now. Understand what the daily differences could mean.

Now it could sound crazy, certainly so. "Woops, I'm going to dial up more security now because it is currently under attack or at risk." Your negative ego — that yamma-yamma voice that always speaks to you (often with your own voice) will tell you that you are crazy, that you have gone off the deep end. It will tell you, "Go out there and manipulate somebody! Go out and guilt-trip somebody! Go out and intimidate somebody! That's how you get more secure." … {laughter} … But, as always, your negative ego lies to you. It will be lying once again.

You have always been able to adjust your *chakras*. You have always been able to be conscious of doing so. Now that your Sirius Connection is active, you can do it more consciously than ever before. The adjustments can be more tangibly meaningful than ever before. Everything is different now.

Electromagnetic Energy

And again, electromagnetic energy has intensified. Marked by greater tectonic activity of earthquakes, by volcanic eruptions, windstorms, electric storms, water storms, and intense heat, the electromagnetics of your world have expanded exponentially. Such energy and its range of manifestations will continue to increase. Oh yes, you are going to see greater storms, greater winds, greater lightning, and massive amounts of flowing water. There will be increasing earthquake and volcanic action. Yes, there will be all kinds of disruptions, including surges of emotional disturbances (violence). But they are not punishment as your chauvinistic eyes would tend to see and your chauvinistic ears would want to hear. No, not punishment. These increases are coming as a way to get that electromagnetic energy into you.

This energy called electromagnetic is essential to the evolution of your brain. It is essential to the evolution of the human species. It is essential to setting up the resonance that can allow the metamorphosis of a new kind of human being. In short, you need this electromagnetic energy or the human race will not survive. It will not survive.

The electromagnetic increases are intended as a help, not a hindrance. If you will absorb the energy, if you will open up to it rather than fearing it and cursing it, so much beauty can unfold. It will stimulate your creativity (part of your personal radiance of resonance), your imagination (part of your attention), and your intuition (part of your intention), and your wisdom (part of your spiritual thirst). Absorb this energy, and it will change you, evolve you. It can trigger the beginning of a metamorphosis.

If you do not absorb it, then the Earth does — thus the physical and emotional phenomena your world is increasingly witnessing. If you do not absorb it, the energy rolls off you and builds up in and about the earth. In time it will release: earthquake, volcano, or attacking environment.

For those of you who are ready for a 12.0 earthquake in California: This will not happen. For those who are waiting for an 8.0, it does not have to happen. You can mitigate it if you will be aware and work at absorbing that energy through your creativity, through your intuition, and through your imagination — letting yourself be more conscious of your intention, attention, and resonance with its radiance.

Be more conscious of your own spiritual hunger and of your *chakra* centers. Use this electromagnetic energy to feed yourself. You will mitigate the physical effects, and not just in your arena.

Before you needed to funnel this kind of energy more directly into your temporal lobes. Now, with your Sirius Connection, you can absorb it directly. When you hear of a massive storm in Indonesia, or a major earthquake in

Malaysia that many might want to see as the beginning of the end, you can mitigate the effect. You can create a quantum leap in your own creative and imaginative nature. And you can confound the experts who are so sure "doom and gloom" is right around the corner.

This is not to say that earthquakes will not happen. They will happen, but they can be mitigated. It is not going against nature. It is changing the vibration, using that same energy in a different way. Energy is energy to be used. Use it in a different way. Absorb it into your own creativity, your own imagination, your own intuition, and your own wisdom. Expand your intention, your attention, and your resonance with that energy. Respond to your spiritual thirst and open to the recalibration of your *chakras*. The electromagnetics can be a part of each of these adventures.

It does not mean you have to grab paper and pencil and suddenly create something. You can use it to change your resonance, your attention, your intention. You can start using these things and confound those experts who are sure this will lead to horrible destruction. Rivers can crest lower than they're expected to. "Gee, I wonder how that happened?" Nobody has to stand up and say, "I did it. I did it." But you can do it.

Then when you hear about these acts that are electromagnetic — violence in cities, emotional violence — you can draw that energy. There is enough of it to go around. You do not have to go looking for it. Draw that energy, and use it to shift your resonance, attention, intention, creativity, imagination, and intuition — and thus mitigate the impact.

Futures Are Creating Your Present ...

Which brings us to the final issue. Futures are now creating your present more completely than ever before. This truth can work against you. The dark potentials: You are wide open now to self-sabotage. The wellspring of traditional failure is lodged in your past. So as you look and watch for potential failure by scouring the past, it can come

Self-sabotage looks like it comes out of the blue. It looks like it has no cause because its cause is not "cause and effect."

at you, unannounced, from the future. It will appear to be failure "out of the blue." Boom.

Well, no. Such failure is not really out of the blue. If you had been looking toward the future, you might well have seen it coming well in advance. The past has ended. By continuing to look there for answers or for anticipated traditional failures, you can get blind-sided with nontraditional failure called sabotage. Whereas the wellspring of traditional failure is in the past, the wellspring of sabotage, especially self-sabotage, is the future.

" ... and I didn't see it coming." ...{laughter}...

Well, that's because it was coming from the other direction.

"Yeah, but I don't know how to deal with looking into the future. What I do know is how to deal with the past. So I'm going to keep looking in the direction of the past!"

It is like looking for the keys under the lamp, even though they were lost over there in the dark, because you can see better over by the lamp, right? ... {laughter} ... That old joke.

Self-sabotage looks like it comes out of the blue. It looks like it has no cause because its cause is not "cause and effect." Rather, it is resonance. It looks like it happened suddenly, without warning, because so much of self-sabotage is a product of a future — not exclusively, but more so — than it is of the past. Sure, secrets and shames can produce self-sabotage. But it's because you throw it into the future.

You see, you are not sabotaging yourself in a loving relationship now because of what someone else did to you in the past. You are sabotaging yourself in a loving relationship now because of what you are doing now and because of what you are intending to do in the future. The cause — the resonance — is in the future and in the present, not in the past.

Now what someone did may keep you from getting into the relationship in the first place. Paying and giving attention to what someone did to you in the past can bring that something into the future and the present, and you can stop yourself from creating even the beginnings of a relationship. You might say, "What future? I never got to first base."

But sabotage happens when you are past first and rounding second. It is then that you break your leg. But see, that is not a product of a past. That is a product of what you do with the past. Too often what you do with it, while throwing it into the future, is called sabotage.

And as the past is ended, the more traditional failures are fewer and farther between. You can still do it. We trust you. ... {laughter} ... You do not have to show us.

But more sabotage is on the horizon, and that is one of the downsides to the fact that the future is more influential now. Self-sabotage becomes a greater threat.

You are going to see people out there in the world sabotaging themselves more frequently than you see them out-and-out fail in the traditional sense. They got the job, and then they embezzled and got caught. Then they ran into the boss's car. They did not fail at getting the job. Only afterwards, they sabotaged themselves, you see? They got into a relationship and then they indulged their infidelity or their unfaithfulness. If they had not been in a relationship, it wouldn't have been called infidelity. But they waited until they had the relationship, and then they were indiscreet. What kind of self-sabotage is this? That's what's coming out of the future.

Similarly, turbulent futures that are already in the pipeline can become more intense and seem to be coming "out of nowhere." It just showed up, or so it seems. People will feel more and more as if they are out of control, and therefore feel a greater need to control, to dominate.

They will convince themselves, and try to convince others, that the world, for some strange, quirky reason, has become more frightening than ever before. Perhaps on a dreary night of depression they laid out a bunch of futures that they never really expected to manifest, but lo and behold, here they come down the chute. Because of the potential threat of self-sabotage and the pipeline of futures, people will feel more out of control and therefore feel more of the need to dominate and control.

However, on the light side, what it means is that the future is wide open. You can create whatever you want to create. It is as though the slate can be clean. And you can purposely create all kinds of wonderful futures, and lay them out there weeks and months in advance.

Maybe not at first, but in time, your Subconscious/ Unconscious will figure out what you are doing. They will soon find that it is fun to do this little Easter egg hunt of creating futures and then going to look for them — going to manifest them. It will be particularly fun since they know where you hid those futures. ... {laughter} ... It is wide open.

What it also means is that all the "Doom and Gloom" does not have to be. It does not matter whether Nostra-damus was right or not. History has ended. The past does not have that impact anymore. You do not have to have any of that reality.

You get to write the rules. You get to decide whether it is going to be a dream, a nightmare, or a mediocrity. Does it take you too long to figure out which answer to choose? "Let's see ... I think I'll take a dream."

You see, it is as if the books that were written so long ago no longer apply. They do not apply. The way it worked does not apply anymore. Therefore, you can create it the way you want it. The slate can be clean. Likewise, you can lay out the most beautiful and most elegant futures. In the pipeline, you can create Optimal Futures.

Now Optimal Futures are not outlandish things like "King of the World." You are not suddenly going to be a zillion-billionaire. ... {laughter} ... That is not an Optimal Future. That's ego fantasy.

But there are ways to create Optimal Futures that you can lay in the pipeline sporadically or purposefully, because the future is now creating the present. You truly can walk away from the past, taking the gifts, the trea-

You see, it is as if the books that were written so long ago no longer apply. They do not apply. The way it worked does not apply anymore. Therefore, you can create it the way you want it.

sures, and the power with you, because those belong to you. And then … let the past go.

And beyond that, just as the dark can mean greater domination, the light can allow you to step into dominion where you can consciously create with an ability to act, co-creating together, side by side, eyeball-to-eyeball with your Unseen Friends. You do not have to keep fixing, fixing, fixing the past, patching it, plugging the holes in it, plugging leaks, hoping no one notices. You can turn your full attention to the future, where there is so much to write, so much to create, so much to change.

Remember, you already believe you can change the future. If you have a past that will not let go, throw it into the future and then change it. What you could not do in the past, you can do in the future.

And the world can be a friendlier place, where you can give and you can love, and where the Elements walk with you. The world can be a place where you and Goddess and God can walk together, not in the physical sense, but in the true metaphysical/spiritual sense. You can open up to that kind of dominion because the future is creating it.

People, you have lived in a world created by others for most of your lifetimes. But now you have a chance to start new. "Boy, if I could just do it all over again knowing what I know now." Your wish just came true.

With the opening of the Vortex of Sirius — with the opening of the Vortex of the Goddess — and with your connection to Sirius, your wish just came true. You can do it all over again knowing what you know now. These things, these things that we talk about today, can be where to begin. Let it begin. Play with these ideas, let them tumble around inside of you. Sometimes, when you least expect it, something wonderful — more than wonderful — happens.

You will use the Light of the Goddess to create a new world with futures filled with magic and miracles. You can also use that same Light to create a brighter, more joyous, reality now.

— Lazaris

You are not alone. You are loved more than you will ever know. If you will allow yourself to receive, what once burdened can now free. What was heavy can become the Light. You are not alone. We love you.

— Lazaris

Resources

The following Lazaris tapes are helpful in working with some of the issues in this chapter or offer further exploration of related areas:

Awakening Our Genius
Utilizing Our Destiny: Consciously Directing Evolution
The Radiance of Resonance Meditation
Discover the Dreamer from Lemuria
Creating a Brilliant Future
Creating Optimal Futures
Healing Ourselves and Our World with Resonance
The Power of Our Chakras: Removing Blockages to Our Success
Weeding Negative Futures & Seeding Positive Futures
Transforming Self-Sabotage into Lasting Success
Reclaiming the Lost Depths of Love: The Missing Ingredient of Miracles

7

Activating & Utilizing the Sirius Connection in Your Daily Living

Shall we sit together under a tree and, between us, dream and vision a world that Imagination forgot? Shall we recreate and create anew the energy and the love that was and once again will be Lemuria? When you are ready. We wait for you. We wait for you at the edge of your reality. For as long as there is Light, we shall love you.

— Lazaris

The secret: Reach for a future waiting to unfold and embrace you rather than retreating into a past waiting to seduce and entrap you.

— Lazaris

What has not happened in over 90,000 years has happened. Astronomically, it cannot happen for another 90,000 years. Yet the Grand Opening of Sirius can happen every day in your heart and mind, in your Soul and Spirit, in the allure and aliveness of your daily living, and in giving voice to your self and Self.

Beyond what this Grand Opening is doing in your world, it is vital to understand how you can more fully activate your connection and how you can more precisely utilize your connections.

We laugh as we say, "You have connections. Use them!"

And now we turn our attentions to technique.

In this time after the Opening of the Vortex, attention and intention come more to the fore; resonance becomes the source of causation; and spiritual hunger and thirst awaken even more than they already have — and awaken in so many about you. Your *chakras* are realigning to a whole new frequency. And indeed electromagnetic energy can be used to boost and to work with your very resonance. With the futures, now so much more impactful, there are ways you can work to create an elegance.

You can continue to use the techniques that you know, from the simplest of manifestation to the most intricate, to create your own reality. Now you approach them with a greater intensity of your own intention, a greater intensity of your own attention, and with an awareness to let in the resonance that it's different now, it's different now. You can have that humility: It is different now.

The futures are far more impactful, far more impactful, than they have ever been. And your brain works differently now. Portions of it are now functioning that never did before. And your DNA is functioning differently now than it ever has. Just sit with that. Just thinking about that — just feeling that — shifts your attention and opens the way for a greater intention to link together pieces of what is your conscious world in alignment with your conscious creation.

With that as a preface, we look at technique.

Resonance

First of all, you can notch up your own overall resonance. Sometimes you can sense: "I'm in the dumps. Yes,

I'm in depressing places. I'm in self-pity places. I'm in martyr places. I know those are low-resonance. I don't have to look them up anywhere." … {laughter} … "Gee, what's my resonance?" Low. That's close enough. … {laughter} …

And if you will not judge yourself, but instead go into and beyond it, you can find the reason you are in martyr. If you are feeling defensive, there is a reason for it, and that reason is because you are defending something. It seems obvious, we know, but that is why people get defensive. … {laughter} … They don't do it for no reason. … "The sun's out, I think I'll be defensive." No, it is always to defend something.

People do not control just for the heck of it, you know? There is always some need they are trying to meet. Martyrhood is an anesthetic, yes, and it is an expression of hostility in its punishing nature, absolutely, but there is always something behind it.

You see, when you are in those resonant places that you know are low, stay out of self-pity — and out of judging yourself. Self-pity and judging shut off any communication. Stay somewhere in between, and let yourself go into the martyrhood, or into the control, or into the defensiveness, into the whatever the low resonance is, and look behind it.

"What am I defending? What am I numbing? What am I avoiding? What am I holding on to, and why?"

In that place, understanding it, you can take your power back. You can take your power back. Then you can let it go, having taken the power, the treasures, and the gifts. Then you can drop the attention from it and shift it to something else.

Then begin to notch your resonance up, to bump it up, to bump it up.

Now you can do that in your meditative Safe Place. You can do that in some special place using your own imagination, using your own creativity, and being inventive about it.

Maybe you would like to get inside the double-tetra-hedron and spin and spin and spin and spin and spin and rotate. In that double-tetrahedron, as you are spinning and rotating, you can disintegrate and suddenly disperse to the whole of the universe. When you come back, you can come back without that low resonance. You can put your martyr out of you. You can put the defensiveness out of you. You spin and rotate and then suddenly you are very nonlocal. You are in the nonlocality of the enfolding energy. And then when you come back together again, you can consciously leave whatever it is out of you. You do not have to let that be part of your molecular structure. Maybe you'll want to go into the future and there let your resonance be notched up.

And that is a technique that you can use. And at first maybe it will not be as effective as it will be later with practice and with a bit of experience, but in time it can be tremendously effective in literally shifting the resonance from one place to another in a very short time — and changing the reality configurations as you do so, changing the reality potentialities as you do so, changing which futures have impact upon you, notching your way up.

Working with Chakra Centers

Certainly you can work with the resonance of your own *chakra* centers. Certainly your Higher Self or one of your Unseen Friends can adjust them. Or you can bask in the Light of Sirius itself, allowing your *chakras* — like radionics dials — to be turned, to be shifted, to be lifted, to be adjusted. Sense your Higher Self reaching in. If you want, we'll be glad to do it. You can work with any of your Unseen Friends. Again, go about it inventively, creatively, finding what feels right.

Perhaps it doesn't make sense to you that you could do that in your Safe Place. Maybe it does make sense to go into the Underworld. Maybe it does make sense to go over the bluff and sit in your Success Cube. Maybe it makes sense to go down by the river and be in a very private place with the willows that weep and the shade and the mottled light.

If that seems appropriate, do it there. You can find the meditative place that feels right for you and adjust your *chakras*.

The Pipeline of Futures

Also you can work with the "Pipeline of Futures". It is most helpful to find a way to go into that future and work with it. You can go into the Underworld. You can go to the Causal Plane. You can use the double-tetrahedron. It is so incredibly effective in teleporting you from the present reality to the futures. In those futures, find the pipeline. Maybe it looks like a clear Lucite pipe. Whatever it looks like to you, it is the pipeline of the futures that are coming.

What's in the pipeline? At first your natural tendency is to be somewhat hesitant. "I don't want to see if there's something horrible there. I don't want see that there's some dread disease, or some terrible accident."

But then you realize, "Wait a minute. Whatever is there, I can change it." Wouldn't it be better to see an auto accident and change it than not to have seen it and manifest it? The short-term gain of avoidance is far outweighed by the long-term reality.

Now that does not mean that you necessarily have to see dreadful horrible deaths and destructions. No, be honest. And in time, as you get used to working with it, you can work very powerfully, very profoundly, to clear the pipeline.

And as you look in the pipeline, you can be very specific. "I am in this relationship with this person, and I'm seeing trouble. There is difficulty we are running into. Let me see what futures are creating this. Let me see what futures are out there. Let me flow into that and find the future. Oh, gosh, this is the future. Six months from now I'm going to realize I was projecting this or fearing that or I was running away from something. But I have found it now, and I can change it in the pipeline."

And once you discover it, allow in the Light of Sirius. Allow in the Goddess. Allow that energy to change what's in the pipeline.

Intercepting & Disconnecting Self-Sabotage

Another technique is what we call Intercepting & Disconnecting.

Now, when you work with self-sabotaging futures, you intercept the potential self-sabotage, you disconnect it, and you release the energy into a new success. And you can do so here.

For example, if you are in a situation where you discover: "Oh, six months from now I'm going to have this huge fight. I can see it, because I can feel it brewing. I can sense it there, so I'm going to disarm it and instead take all that energy that otherwise would have been a fight and create an incredibly close, intimate experience."

Intercept those futures. Now this might have been a somewhat airy-fairy technique a few years ago, but now, because everything's different, because the Vortex is open, you can work with it, though maybe not exclusively.

Maybe you also want to use the techniques that you are very familiar with. Certainly so, if you recognize that it's your martyr, you may want to use the techniques you know to deal with that. But you may also want to create a variation using the future techniques to begin to stretch your experience and expertise with intercepting and disconnecting futures.

The Light of Sirius

And of course there is always the Light of Sirius itself. Since the Opening, that resonance of Sirius is inside you. Perhaps you will want to connect with it by stepping outside at night and looking up to the heavens and locating Sirius, just off there to the left of Orion's Belt — that twinkling star — and calling upon it, sensing it, opening to it.

Perhaps you will do the same thing in a meditation where you are sitting on a mound of earth and looking up into the night sky, sensing it, letting it come, calling on Sirius ... "In the name of Sirius, in the name of the Goddess, in the name of ..." An abstract, phenomenally powerful, technique.

[Ed. Note: Techniques for the "Skill of Claiming" and the "Art of Demanding" are on the tape *Reclaiming the Lost Depths of Love: The Missing Ingredient of Miracles.*]

Journal Pages

Notching Resonance

(... thoughts and feelings about the Possible and its power ... resonance that you are raising and the results you are experiencing.)

Journal Pages

The Pipeline of Futures

Optimal Futures

There is a technique for creating Optimal Futures.

Now we are not saying optimum meaning "the most incredible of all." There can be many Optimal Futures. If you go for optimum, it gets competitive. You know, which one is better? And ... "Could I come up with a better one?" There can many Optimal Futures.

The idea here is that you are going to create these Optimal Futures, and you are going to lay them within your Radiance of Resonance. And they will start having impact now, long before you would ever manifest them, for as a conduit of that future, they change you now.

Now, admittedly, this technique takes time, it takes thought, it takes work. So it is not something you can just throw together.

There are several components, but you can take your time. And you work on it over a period of days or weeks. Not every day, not all week for weeks. You work on it, maybe a little bit now, and a little bit a couple of days from now, coming back after you have thought about, it after you've worked with it. "Yeah, made some changes there."

So again, respect yourself and don't just throw it together. The goal here is not to get it done as soon as possible or to do a great many of them ... "I've got a book full of Optimal Futures. I got 20 or 30 of them this afternoon alone. I just sat down and buzz-sawed through them." ... {laughter} ...

That is probably self-sabotage. ... {laughter} ...

Now, an Optimal Future has several characteristics:

First of all, Optimal Futures involve challenge and skill. They involve challenge that somehow engages or calls upon your strength, your power, and your talent. Optimal Futures call upon your creativity, your confidence (your ability to cope), and your expertise as well.

An Optimal Future involves a certain level of skill that presents a challenge — not struggle, but a challenge — an interesting, curious, wonderful challenge. And that challenge involves or in some way engages some of your strength, some of your power, some of your particular talent. Challenge engages it and then takes your strength, your power, or your talent to the edge and then … just beyond the edge. Challenge calls for new learning within the skills you have; it calls for developing new skills.

When you say you are going to be the quadrillion-billion-dillionaire of the world, there is no skill there. There is no challenge there, because the goal has become meaningless. There is no way to engage your strengths, power, or talent.

Second: It is important that an Optimal Future involve complexity and attention. That is, in order to do this skill, in order to do this task that involves skill and challenge, it engages your full attention. It cannot be something you do on automatic. As well, it must have complexity. It must work with the differentiation and integration that is complexity.

Complexity exists when you allow something to be an expression of your individuality as well as your oneness or Oneness.

Now complexity is often seen as difficulty. It does not have to be difficult. Intricate, yes. Involved, yes. But not necessarily difficult.

Complexity exists when you allow something to be an expression of your individuality as well as your oneness or Oneness. When an Optimal Future expresses your uniqueness as well as your sameness, it has complexity. Complexity involves your individuality, your uniqueness, your signature, your autonomy, as well as your partnership, as well as the "together energy" you have with others, as well as your oneness and Oneness. Such partnership, togetherness, and oneness may involve your spiritual community and spiritual family more than your biological and chemical family. Your spiritual family is developed not by chemistry and biology but by character, by personal and spiritual character.

Therefore, an Optimal Future is not something you do totally alone — or if it is, it gets passed on to or is involved with others.

Also, whatever it is, you want to become totally absorbed in it while you are doing it. Not obsessed, but absorbed.

And, you see, there are those of you doing things in your life now that already involve a certain amount of skill and challenge, and which give you the chance to express your individuality as well as your oneness with another. Some of you are working in sporting activities. Some of you are working in creative projects that are purely hobby but are nonetheless beautifully creative. Some of you are in relationships where you are taking the skill and the challenge of intimacy, love, and caring that calls upon your strength, power, and talent as well as your creativity, confidence, and expertise. That gives you the opportunity to be fully yourself and a partner with another. The groundwork is there; you have already begun.

Third: An Optimal Future needs to have clarity — specific and clear goals, short-term and long-term, immediate and eventual.

An example: You see yourself having an Optimal Future in which you compose music. That involves a skill. Certainly it involves a challenge, because no matter how talented you may be, such composition calls upon and stretches that talent. It involves challenge. It involves skill. It calls upon your strengths. It calls upon your power of vision and creativity. It calls upon your talent. And it requires confidence: "I have confidence, a sense that in that future I can do it with the expertise."

And it is intricate, complex. It involves you, but it also involves others who will listen to or who will play or who will enjoy this music.

And to that end, it takes your attention. When you are focusing on this composition, you can see yourself totally engaged, totally involved.

And there is a clarity. There are goals in mind. You want to write so many measures every day. Or you want to get the first movement done by a certain time. There is a goal of completion, a goal of achievement, a goal of accomplishment that is clear.

Fourth: An Optimal Future needs to involve choice, the choice to take charge of the situation, to exercise control *in* the situation, rather than having to be in control *of* the situation. You can exercise control in the situation in varying degrees of intensity. Rather than having to control the entire situation or environment — rather than having to control it — you can exercise control within the situation or within the environment. Perhaps it is easier to sense this as taking charge of your reality rather than controlling other people and things in your reality.

You have that choice: to intensify or to lighten up, to work faster or to work slower, to let it ebb and flow. You have that sense of choice.

Fifth: An Optimal Future needs to have a continuum of feedback, short-term and long-term feedback, a system of gratification and reward, where some of the feedback is immediate. Going back to our composer, you have set the goal: Today you want to get this many measures done, this many minutes. This portion has been a stickler. Yes, you would get immediate feedback from that. Now this is a future. You are not doing it, but you can see that it has the opportunity of immediate feedback. It has that immediate gratification, that immediate reward.

The sixth quality it must involve is commitment and centering, where you are absolutely committed to doing it, to being engaged in it, to being involved in it — a total commitment in the moment, in the now, centered, where you have to give it all your focus now. You cannot be distracted. You want to create it in such a way that you can be totally centered and totally committed.

Finally, an Optimal Future needs to stretch you beyond your self-consciousness so that your Conscious Self can emerge. Ironically and paradoxically, being self-conscious is never your Self and it is never being conscious.

An Optimal Future is bigger and grander than you are, and because of that, it lifts and engages you such that you lose all sense of self-consciousness. You forget the cameras are rolling. (In fact, they are not rolling.) With an Optimal

It may well be called a moment of ecstasy, where you are in a euphoria, in a sense of unity, of oneness, beyond space and time. Sacred, ineffable, a self-transcendent moment.

Future, you are not conscious of people watching. You are not conscious of what they think, of whether they care, of what they are deciding. You don't even know they are there. You are so engaged that it stretches you beyond being self-conscious.

It may well be called a moment of ecstasy, where you are in a euphoria, in a sense of unity, of oneness, beyond space and time. Sacred, ineffable, a self-transcendent moment. You let your self-consciousness gó so that in that transcendent moment, in that self-transcendent time, the real you, the true you, the Self that you really are, can emerge.

Now admittedly, these characteristics of an Optimal Future take some thinking and feeling. They take some playing around with.

Now putting together an Optimal Future calls upon what? It calls up challenge and skill. It calls upon complexity and attention. It also calls upon clarity. Beyond clarity, an Optimal Future calls upon choice. Choice is pivotal to Optimal Futures. And then there are continuums — continuums of feedback. There is commitment and centering. Finally, an Optimal Future calls upon consciousness and upon being conscious.

With all of this woven together — some threads thicker, some thinner — you can create a fabric of the future that can affect you now. Woven together to create an Optimal Future, these energies will automatically raise your resonance.

As you finalize the creation of an Optimal Future, to make it complete and whole, you digest it, and you project it.

Let it in. Let it in. Imagine yourself composing, following our previous example, or imagine yourself climbing that mountain or fulfilling the goal whatever it might be. You imagine yourself engaged in this or that activity. Imagine yourself having that home where you can be and do all these creative projects. Imagine it.

And as you create it, it is raising your resonance. As you imagine it, as you digest it, it becomes a part of you. You sense it. You feel it. You smell it and touch it in your imagination.

Then you project it out there into what we call your Radiance of Resonance — that wedge of the futures you can experience. OK?

Here is your resonance now. After working with creating an Optimal Future, it is maybe moved up a few notches. Now you are feeling pretty good about yourself. As a matter of fact, you're feeling very positively, drawing in a more valuable reality than you were before you put this Optimal Future together.

Now you digest it. You feel it. You let yourself taste it. What does it taste like? What does it smell like? What does it feel like? You are notching up now just a little bit. Not enough that anybody might notice any difference, but you are still notching up.

Once you have digested it, throw it out there. Project it out into your future. How far? Well, it depends. If this is an Optimal Future for when you retire from work and sell your property and move to the country, it may be 20 or 30 years from now — even though between now and then you may change it.

That does not matter. You still digest it and throw it out there. Throw it out there somewhere within the Radiance — obviously on the upper end of the your Radiance of Resonance.

Your Optimal Future, by its very projection, is starting to have impact on you now. It will start immediately to have impact on you. Subtle, yes. It may cause you to feel more optimistic about something, or your programming around some issue may be more effective. Whatever, it is drawing you toward it, toward that Optimal Future.

Now if you have four or five of them out there, they are each going to draw you — not necessarily any faster, but more deeply. It does not mean you're going to be 65 years old any sooner, you see? ... {laughter} ... But it'll draw you more deeply.

Now, if you want to really have it come in more deeply, you can do one of two things.

You can consciously start developing that skill more fully and exercising the challenge. You can start developing that complexity and that attention even now. You can bring the clarity into your current reality. You can exercise that particular skill, that particular challenge, or that particular complexity. You can start exercising that in direct activity.

You see, when you are in that Optimal Future, you want to be doing some specific thing. You do not necessarily know how to do that yet, but it has always been there as a dream that you've had. So you think and feel, "It seems like that would be such an incredible reality, to do woodworking, to carve. But I don't know how to do that." So you are going to start developing the skill now — preparing, learning, taking steps, maybe taking a class here, reading a book there.

It's anchoring. It is not anchoring that future to you, it is anchoring you to that future. We should say that again: It is not anchoring that future to you, it is anchoring you to that future.

You start developing the particular skill now, and it will anchor you and pull you to that Optimal Future more deeply, more richly, changing the reality along the way more significantly.

Now the other way: Maybe that particular Optimal Future is something that cannot really happen until out there in the more distant future. There is no real way you could go about developing the skill or challenge. It is just not an appropriate thing to do, or it would take too much of your time and energy right now in your world.

So the other way you can anchor your current reality to the Optimal Future is to find something else that you can do now — not upon the same specific challenge-skill, but upon some other challenge-skill and complexity-attention.

It's anchoring. It is not anchoring that future to you, it is anchoring you to that future.

It will not have the same clear goals, but it will have some clear goals. And there is always choice. With that choice, you may not be able to exercise the same kind of control in the situation or may not be able to take charge in the environment, but you can exercise some taking charge. Though practice is over, you can still develop ability.

This "something" may not afford the same feedback or continuum for it, but it will have feedback in a continuum of rewards and gratifications. And it will involve that sense of commitment, not to the Optimal Future, but to the quite separate activity you are working on now. And you can still become so engaged that, while losing your self-consciousness, you become more conscious of self and Self.

It may be that you have an Optimal Future out here that has to do with more academic concerns. But right now you express it through playing tennis. Challenge-Skill? Complexity-Attention? Certainly so. You cannot be thinking about what you had for breakfast, who you are going to see later, or whether it is awfully hot. You must be right there, in the moment. You must be intense. Clarity and Choice? Continuum of feedback? Of course, these are very present ... after every volley. ... {laughter} ...

Does it involve that sense of commitment, that sense of absolute, centered commitment in the moment? And do you escape yourself? Yes, if you are not worried about your hemline or whether your shoes are white enough, or whatever. You lose yourself. You lose yourself, your self-consciousness. And a more real you emerges. It can. Not always, but it can.

With this variation, while in your 20s, an activity like playing tennis can link you, can connect you, to an Optimal Future that has nothing to do with playing tennis or with any other such physical activity. Tennis in your 20s can link you to an Optimal Future that you plan to play out in your 30s, 50s, 70s or beyond.

Being conscious of what you are doing, being conscious of making this link and then actually making it, can nudge and push your resonance. It is going to lift your resonance, because it involves the attention and the intention.

And it involves the qualities of resonance raising from clarity to creativity.

When you start digesting it, it nudges your resonance a little further. When you project it out there, it nudges you further. And that can be enough.

Then every so often let yourself digest it again. Ponder it. Savor it. Daydream about it. Dream about it in your meditations or in your night dreams.

As you do this, you will start creating Optimal Experiences and Optimal Futures, and the link can be phenomenal. It can generate successes that seem not to have anything to do with what you are doing.

You see, it has impact, shifting your resonance — not just your resonance about the Optimal Future, but your resonance now. That Optimal Future may be very involved in healing a malady you have now. Not so that you can hurry up and achieve the Optimal Future, but so you can move your Radiance of Resonance now.

An example: "Here's my Radiance of Resonance now, which includes X disease. And through creating this Optimal Future I have nudged my resonance up to here where now that disease X is outside the wedge or scope of energy created by my resonance. Because disease X is no longer within my radiance of resonance, I can now let it go. Therefore it goes away."

The particular Optimal Future that nudged the resonance, in this example, had nothing to do with curing or healing the specific malady in question. The Optimal Future may have been something very different from anything to do with disease or illness. Yet it still lifted the resonance to a level where the disease or illness could not maintain itself. The radiance of that resonance was too high to hold the disease or illness.

Unable to stand the resonance — even though that Optimal Future had nothing to do with that particular health concern — the disease and the reality around it can change now.

And what other futures are here in this radiance of your resonance, in the wedge of your resonance? When your radiance of resonance moves up, futures that are all along the wedge shift and change. And it becomes like magic, very much like magic, so much like it that it probably is magic. ... {laughter} ...

Now that the Vortex is open, now that the past has ended its bitter grip and control, now that practice is over, everything is different. Not "can be" — is different. You can make it suspiciously the same, but it is different.

Journal Pages

Challenge - Skill

Complexity - Attention

Journal Pages

Clarity

Choice

Journal Pages

Continuum of Feedback

Commitment

Journal Pages

Conscious Self

(Letting go of self-consciousness to become conscious of Self.)

Meditation

In meditation, again open to the energy of Sirius, to your connection. Call upon Sirius and the archetypal energy that Sirius represents. Call upon the Goddess through this gateway, this portal to Her realm. It is your right. It is your right.

You know, we have talked so often about that stellar heritage. And there is magic in the telling. Let yourself remind yourself. Let your self remember (and re-member) the story of Sirius and of the Vortex of the Goddess. There is magic in the telling. That magic is your right.

What of your stellar heritage? It is either Sirius or Pleiades. No, it's not Orion. … {laughter} … Even if there is an Orion connection, that connection is either Pleiades/Orion or Sirius/Orion. So your stellar heritage is Sirius, or it is Pleiades. If not, you would not have found any interest in wanting to deal with the Sirius Connection, you see? It would not have interested you. Call upon that heritage. It is your inheritance. It is your right. Claim it. Declare it.

You see, this is not the first time you have been a Map Maker. It's not a job assignment that is handed out like karma. "Who wants maps?" … {laughter} …

It is a quality of who you are. It is part of your nature. It is your destiny — chosen, yes, but then only Mapmakers choose to be Mapmakers. In a planet full of people, in a universe full of consciousnesses, there are relatively very few of you overall. But enough. …

And so it is …

There is so much more we could talk about in and around this topic. Your Sirius Connection is complex, and it is deep. It is also always unfolding, becoming, and being more. There is so much we could say. But perhaps, for now, we have said enough. …

~

Until we have the opportunity to work with you, be it in workshops, in Blendings, or in meditation, we shall close, and we shall do so, to each of you and all of you, with love — oh yes, with love — with love, and peace.

LAZARIS

Appendix

Lazaris Seminars & Tapes
Books & Music
Calendars & Journals

Lazaris Seminars

In the years since 1974, when Lazaris began channeling through Jach Pursel, his only channel, he has created an ever-expanding number of avenues for metaphysical and spiritual growth. Among them are the delightful Lazaris Seminars.

Lazaris conducts seminars frequently in San Francisco, Los Angeles, Atlanta, Orlando, Newark, NJ, and occasionally in other cities as the schedule allows.

Ranging from Evenings with Lazaris to One-Days, Weekends, and three- and four-day Intensives, they provide wonderful in-depth explorations of everything from clearing personal blockages to exciting emerging metaphysical and spiritual opportunities. During longer seminars channel Jach Pursel sometimes provides a one-hour discussion session called *Some Time with Jach.*

The Jach & Lazaris Room on CompuServe

In the New Age Forum on CompuServe there are both library and message sections called the *Jach & Lazaris Room.* There is a wealth of information available — Lazaris articles and messages Lazaris writes specifically for the forum — and many delightful threads of exploration going on. It's incredible fun. Join us! To find us, log onto CompuServe and "GO LAZARIS" from basic services.

Lazaris' Mailing List

Concept: Synergy organizes the seminars and publishes the Lazaris tapes and books. If you would like to be on our mailing list and receive information about Lazaris seminars and notification of new books and tapes, please call us at 1-800/678-2356.

Personal Growth Tapes

Tapes from the Evenings with Lazaris, three hours of discussion, tools and techniques, and a guided meditation.

1996: The Year of Wonder
1996: The Mastery & Artistry of 1996, July - December
1996: Underlying Truths: Magical Formulas To Master 1996
Abundance & Prosperity: The Skill
Accelerating the Pace of Manifesting Success
Accessing the Incredible Force of Love
Activating Miraculous Success
Alleviating Your Life Lesson & Letting It Serve You
The Artistry of Loving: Creating & Manifesting
Awakening Our Genius
Backdrop of Success/Creating the New Fabric
Balance: Releasing the Full Self
Being Loved
Beyond Struggle: The Magic of Being Good Enough
Busting & Building Image
Busting Free: Beyond the Need To Control
Coming Home
Consciously Creating Success
Crafting the Life You've Always Wanted
Creating & Cultivating Your Spiritual Family
Creating a Brilliant Future
Creating, Building & Keeping Intimate Relationships
Crisis of Martyrhood
Crystals: The Power & Use
Developing Self-Confidence
Discovering the Adult
Discovering Your Subconscious
Dominion at Work: Engaging the Elements
The Elegance of Abundance
Ending Guilt
Ending Loneliness
Ending the Pain
Ending Self-Punishment
Ending Self-Sabotage
Ending Shame, Part I: Infancy
Ending Shame, Part II: Psychic Contracts of Pain
Ending Shame, Part III: Those Adolescent Years

Continued on next page ...

Personal Growth Tapes ...

Ending Shame, Part IV: Adult Shame
Ending Your Addiction to the Past
Escaping the Entrapment of "Perfection"
Escaping the Suffocating Web of Anxiety
Expanding Success Exponentially
Explore the Wonder: A New Kind of Intimacy/A New Kind of Love
Finally Accepting Self: Being Fully Loved
Freedom from Self-Pity
Freedom from the Unspeakable: Jealousy, Envy, Rage
The Gentle Walk: Step-by-Step Intimacy with Your Higher Self
Giving Voice to Your Soul
The Great Circle of Love: Magic & Miracles
Harmony: The Power Vortex
Harnessing the Power: Magically Ending Martyrhood
Healing Ourselves and Our World with Resonance
Healing: The Nature of Health, I
Healing: The Nature of Health, II
Healing the Scars of the Past, Charting the Future
I Deserve!
Incredible Force of Forgiveness
Inner Peace
In Search of Miracles
Intimacy
Intuition
The Journey Unfolds: Coming Home, Part II
Letting More Love into Your Life
Living Magically Every Day
The Lost Treasures of Joy
The Magic of Joy
The Magic of Receiving: A New Dimension of Success
Making This Your Last Lifetime
Moving Beyond Guilt & Fear:
     New Entanglements with Old Names
Mysterious Power of Chakras
The Mystery & Magic of Co-Creation
Negative Ego: Ending the Co-Dependency
New Dimensions of Joy
New Dynamics of Processing & Programming
New Maps to More Elegant Futures
Our Secret Prison: Discover/Break the Dark Law
Personal Depth: The Journey of Health, Wealth & Success
Power of Dominion
The Power of Our Chakras: Removing Blockages to Our Success

The Powerful Secret of Reflection:
"With Little or No Effort At All ..."
Programming What You Want
Prosperity & Abundance in the 1990s
Reality Creation: The Basics
Reclaiming the Lost Depths of Love:
The Missing Ingredient of Miracles
Reclaiming Your Lost Depth of Soul: Awakening Your Spirit
Relationships That Work: Creating the Next Level
Secrets of Success in the Remaining Years of the Millennium
Secrets To Changing Anything in Your Life — Instantly
Self-Esteem
Self Worth / Self-Respect
The Sirius Connection: What It Can Mean in Your Daily Life
(no meditation)
Standing on the Verge:
Elegant Visions Creating Magical Successes
Stop Feeling Not Good Enough
Transforming Negativity: Enemies into Allies
Transforming Personal Fear into Amazing Success
Transforming Self-Sabotage into Lasting Success
The True Magic & Power of Waking Up & Staying Awake
The Unseen Friends
Turning Potential into Successful Achievement
Utilize the Unknown Powers of the Magical Child
Utilizing Our Destiny: Consciously Directing Evolution
Utilizing Night Dreams To Create Greater Success
Utilizing the Incredible Mystery & Magic of Expectation
Utilizing the Power of Choice To Generate Profound Change
Waking the Magician: Sacred Return to Oneness
Winning the Manifestation Game
Winning: New Tools To Get What You Really Want
Working with Your Shadow:
An Imperative on the Spiritual Path
Your Future Self

Lazaris Blank Journals

Quotes by Lazaris, covers by Gilbert Williams. Two cover choices:

"Gathering Place" Cover
"Mist Angel" Cover

The Red Label Series

Meditation tapes to re-pattern your subconscious to allow more beneficial realities in specific areas.

Handling Depression/Loneliness
Happiness/Peace
High Energy/Enthusiasm
Improved Health/Balance/Harmony
Integrity/Honesty
Monetary Success/Personal Success
Personal Power/Power & Dominion
Productivity/Impeccability
Reduced Sleep/Improved Sleep
Reducing Fear/Worry/Stress
Self-Confidence/Self-Awareness
Self-Love/Love

Lazaris Books

Please see the title page for books in other languages.

The Sacred Journey: You and Your Higher Self
The Sacred Journey Meditation Tapes
The Sirius Connection
Working with Your Shadow: An Imperative on the Spiritual Path

Lazaris & Peny Tapes

Discussions on a myriad of fascinating subjects from the delightful Evenings with Lazaris and Peny, plus one tape made "at home."

Feb. '92 Palm Beach Evening
April '91 Palm Beach Evening
April '86 Evening
July '86 Evening
November '86 Evening
SF March '87 Evening
LA March '87 Evening
At Home with Lazaris & Peny

Calendar

Quotes by Lazaris, art work by Gilbert Williams.

The Lazaris-Gilbert Williams Calendar (published annually)

Lazaris Videos

Full-color videos in VHS and PAL, two hours, all with meditations. Audio versions of all the videos are also available.

Achieving Intimacy & Loving Relationships
Awakening the Love
Developing a Relationship with Your Higher Self
Developing Self-Confidence
Forgiving Yourself
The Future: How To Create It
Listening to the Whispers
The Mysteries of Empowerment
Overcoming Fear of Success
Personal Excellence
Personal Power & Beyond
Releasing Negative Ego
Secrets of Manifesting What You Want, Part I
Secrets of Manifesting What You Want, Part II
Spiritual Mastery: The Journey Begins
Unconditional Love
Unlocking the Power of Changing Your Life

Lazaris Discussions

AIDS: A Compassionate Exploration
Healing Hurt / The Keys of Happiness
Lazaris Talks about AIDS with Louise L. Hay's Group
On Releasing Anger / On Releasing Self-Pity
On Releasing Guilt / On Receiving Love
Lazaris Talks with Vietnam Veterans
The Synergy of Trust
Beyond the Threshold / Editing the Film
Cleaning Chakras / Pituitary-Pineal Meditation
The Goddess Series, Part I
The Goddess Series, Part II
Handling Menstruation

Tapes for Children & Teenagers

Lazaris with Beky Carter.

Relaxation and Self-Love/Good Health and Chakras (Age 4-10)
Expressing Emotions/Communicating with Parents (Age 4-10)
Expressing Emotions/Communicating with Parents (Age 11+)
Self-Forgiveness/Self-Love (Age 11+)

Letting More Love into Your Life

Techniques and meditations from Weekends, Intensives, and One-Days.

The Pillar of Light Meditation
The Depth of Chakra Meditation
The Tree of Love Meditation
The Circle of Love Meditation
The Circle of Forgiveness Meditation
The Reconnecting with Emotional Depth Meditation
The Igniting the Essence Meditation
The Double-Tetrahedron Technique and Meditation
The Tonal Creation and Manifestation Technique
The Radiance of Resonance Meditation
Weeding Negative Futures and Seeding Positive Futures
Creating Optimal Futures

Connecting with Lazaris Tapes

A special series of 30-minute tapes, many with 28-day processes, for awakening, building dreams, and deepening a connection with Lazaris.

Accepting the Gifts of the Metaphysician
Allowing the Fun
Awakening Your Brain
Building & Achieving Destiny
Building Your Personal Dream, Part I
Building Your Personal Dream, Part II
Choosing Your Own Lessons
A Cherished Secret of Success: Resonance
Embracing Power
Empowering Your Imagination
Enhancing Visualization
Feeling More of Lazaris' Love: Blending
Getting More Magic Out of Your Meditations
Healing the Child Within
Healing the Adolescent Within
Hearing the Music ... Allowing the Magic
Letting Yourself Be Loved: Allowing Lazaris' Love
Loving Better, Loving More Deeply
Loving Someone More
The Magic of Solitude
Mind Meld: Higher Self
The Power & Beauty of Self-Acceptance
Receiving Clearer, More Helpful Answers in Meditation
Receiving the Healing from Your Higher Self
Renewing Chakras
Sharpening Tools: Awakening Desires

The Accelerated Journey Series

One-hour discussions with meditations, to accelerate your Spiritual Journey Home.

Breaking & Replacing the Dark Shield of Negativity
Building the Dream Your Higher Self Has for You
Chakra Link: You and Your Higher Self
The Crisis Tape
Discovering Your Personal Strengths and Unique Powers
Discover the Dreamer from Lemuria
Embracing Your Higher Self: Receiving the Love
The Evening Tape
Finding Your Bottom Line
Finding Your Own Peace
Freedom from Karma
Freedom from the Past
The Goddess: Beginning to Receive Her
High Magic: The Ritual of Receiving
Initiations of Magic
Longevity: The Healing Technique
The Magic of Our Spiritual Ancestry
The Mists of Manifestation
A More Powerful Causal Plane
The Morning Tape
Opening the Magic Door
Preparing for Achievement
Releasing Your Dreams & Visions into the World
Stop Negativity in Its Tracks
Unlocking Your Unconscious
Utilizing Solstice & Equinox Energy

Music Tapes ... Cassettes

Music written especially for Lazaris and featured in many of the Lazaris meditations on tape.

Prelude to Lazaris
Lazaris: A Spark of Love
Lazaris Remembers Lemuria *(also available as a CD)*
Lazaris & the Dolphins
Journey with Lazaris
The Love of Lazaris
Through the Vortex with Lazaris